The SOUPBOX COOKBOOK

The SOUPBOX COOKBOOK

Sensational Soups for Healthy Living

JAMIE TAERBAUM and DRU MELTON, founders of the
✓ Voted the best soup in Chicago on Citysearch

Race Point
PUBLISHING

A division of Book Sales, Inc.
276 Fifth Avenue Suite 206
New York, New York 10001

ISBN-13: 978-1-93799-406-8

Photography by Bill Bettencourt
Food styling by Lynne Aloia

Printed in China

2 4 6 8 10 9 7 5 3 1

www.racepointpub.com

This book is dedicated to our great and loyal customers who have kept us in business for the past seventeen years. Also to Betty Ann, Carol Ann, Bernadine, Pearl, and the rest of our families; eating with you made us better cooks.

CONTENTS

Ahh soup. How to describe something with so many personal meanings and interpretations? Soup is something familiar to everyone. Soup is served everywhere; from the poor fringes of society to the high-rent districts in exclusive zip codes. Everyone remembers a few choice soups from a favorite restaurant, vacation or meal at a relative's house. Soup is more than food. It's friendly. It's a joy.

Soup transports people back in time. It takes us to Grandma's kitchen, our childhood home, happy places. It fills the house with good, rich and appealing smells. It's homey, something made with love, full of flavor and the memories of the people who made it. We eat soup for special occasions, fancy meals as well as sickness or when we run out of money. From quick and simple broths to rich and time-consuming stews and chowders, soup satisfies with great flavors, transforming simple water to pure bliss. Soup is the one-size-fits-all dish that's capable of satisfying many palates at once.

So what does soup mean to me? In a word soup means "Comfort." In more words it means, "Home. Satisfaction. Nutritious and nurturing." It can be highbrow and low end, sometimes at the same time; glamorous or humble depending on your whim. The right soup can brighten your day. Soup is equally at home as a first course or an entrée; few other foods can lay the same claim. What other dishes have infiltrated our family vernacular so thoroughly? Grandma's Chicken Noodle. Dad's (In) famous Four-alarm Chili. Uncle Bill's Beef Barley. Mom's Immortal Tomato Soup, served with a smile and a piping hot grilled cheese. What pleasures! These are the memories of legend, the link to the little boy or girl we used to be.

Soup means so many things to so many people for good reason. Soup brings a home cook or a professional chef easy and quick means to a satisfying end; that special moment when the spoon hits the tongue and the face brightens with a smile.

SOUPBOX

Soupbox took us all by surprise. Back when the store first opened, it was called Icebox, and we only made Icyfruit, which is sort of like Italian Ice but is all natural with fresh fruit mixed in and no artificial colors or flavors. Soup came along later as we tried to think of something we could offer that would be as unique as Icyfruit and a means to make rent during the cold, gray Chicago winter. We talked and talked, brainstormed and argued, pouted and then talked some more. Somehow, someway, someone said, "Soup." Many people claim they came up with the idea. To this day I couldn't tell you if it was Jamie's mother Betty Ann or the guy from the stereo store down the street or our sales rep George who we still buy fruit and produce from to this day. And quite frankly it doesn't matter. What matters is having something that grows, breathes and ages before your eyes. Something that we built up over time. Something that became part of the lives of the Soupbox's neighbors.

To this day I remain convinced that free samples are what kept us in business. My cooking training and management skills helped. Jamie's incredible knack for catching trends kept us on track. But the key was free samples. Back when we first opened, people would walk by and laugh; tell us we'd be out of business in a few months. Things changed when we started meeting those same people with a tray of hot, delicious samples; giving away our soup gave us a foothold and their allegiance; we haven't looked back since!

Small business is the engine that drives our country. Rarely will you see a large conglomerate company or chain coming into the market-place with new and edgy ideas because they don't want to take risk. Being young and somewhat dumb, we didn't fear risk or failure.

Instead Jamie found the storefront and financed the rehab by charging up credit cards. And it worked. I would add that few jobs are as difficult and time consuming as owning and running your own business. At the same time, few jobs are as rewarding. Growing with and learning how to run a small business in Chicago has been one of the chief accomplishments of my life. I took over the Broadway store when I was just 23 years old. Seventeen years later we've grown, changed and learned a lot with lessons on every possible topic you can imagine: taxes and the importance of a top-notch accountant; interpersonal relationships and how much good communication skills can help; the need to treat everyone around you with love and respect; the unequivocal commitment to quality ingredients; the temerity to never cut corners; and the sheer bull stubbornness that is my refusal to fail. All of these important life lessons have come to me through Soupbox. Blind dumb luck or just rewards—it doesn't matter; getting up tomorrow morning and getting ready for the lunch rush does.

We pride ourselves in our soups, work hard to make them great and are excited to share our best recipes with our customers and anyone who loves great soup. It's a privilege for us, and we hope it will be a joy for you. Serving delicious soup is our pleasure.

CHAPTER ONE

VA VA VEGETABLES

I just love vegetable soups. Coming from a small Midwestern town, I didn't taste a mango until I was twelve so when I got into cooking school I desperately was looking for new and different flavors and tastes. I experimented with all kinds of vegetables and all sorts of exotic sauces. I loved all of them, but often found myself yearning for the simple and clean tastes of a straight-forward garden vegetable soup. The flavors sparkle and the clean, clear broth is the perfect savory complement. And they are so easy to make. It's good food at its purest.

To cook a great vegetable soup you need to pay careful attention to the aromatics, the carrots, celery, onion, garlic and spices. A good soup is like a good house, you have to build it from the foundation. Make sure you sauté the aromatics carefully and wait until you bring out the fragrance which will flavor the oil and create that flavor foundation. The great thing about soup is its simplicity. You could take all the ingredients for any of the recipes, throw them into a pot and 30 to 50 minutes later you'll get soup. However, if you introduce the onions, celery, carrots or whatever you are starting with to heated oil or butter, and cook until translucent, you release great tasting oils that add big flavor. Heat transforms the taste; if you bite into a raw onion, it tastes bright and sharp, but if you slowly sauté it, you can make it sweet.

AUTUMN MEMORIES ROASTED BUTTERNUT SQUASH SOUP WITH SAGE AND APPLE

The sage and apple add a nice and fresh twist to this fall favorite.
This soup takes longer than most to prepare but is worth it.

Ingredients

1 butternut squash, peeled and cut into 2 inch chunks

2 medium carrots, quartered

1 medium onion, quartered

2 Gala apples, cored and peeled and cut into quarters

3 cloves garlic

2 tbsp olive or canola oil

2 bay leaves

1 tsp dried thyme

1 tsp dried sage

½ tsp salt

¼ tsp white pepper

32 oz vegetable stock

1 cup heavy cream

Cooking Instructions

Preheat the oven to 425 degrees. In a large mixing bowl toss the squash, carrots, onion, apples, garlic and the dried herbs in the olive oil and spread them evenly on a foil-lined baking sheet. Roast in the oven until the squash is tender, approximately 35-45 minutes. The vegetables should be tender and lightly browned. Remove them from the oven and transfer the contents of the baking sheet to a large stockpot set over medium heat.

Add the vegetable stock, bring the contents to a simmer and cook for 15 minutes to allow the flavors to marry. After 15 minutes, remove the soup from the heat and purée with a food processor in batches. If the soup is too thick, add a bit more stock. Add the heavy cream. (Be sure to remove from heat first.) Taste the soup and adjust seasonings with salt and pepper as needed.

fry sage leaves + add on top

Serves 6 | PREP TIME: 30 minutes. COOK TIME: 1½ hours.

MUSHROOM BARLEY SOUP

This is one of our most popular soups at the stores.

Ingredients

8 oz or one cup white button mushrooms, sliced

8 oz or one cup shitake mushrooms, sliced

1 medium onion, diced

1 medium carrot, diced

2 stalks celery, diced

2 tbsp olive oil

2 cloves garlic, minced

1 tsp thyme

2 bay leaves

48 oz vegetable stock

½ cup pearled barley

Salt and fresh ground pepper to taste

VEGAN FAVORITE

Cooking Instructions

In a large stockpot with a lid, sweat the mushrooms, onion, carrot, and celery in the olive oil over medium heat for 10 minutes. Stir often. Add the garlic, thyme and bay leaves and cook till fragrant, about one minute longer. Add the vegetable stock, cover and bring the soup to a simmer. Add the pearled barley and cook for 35-45 minutes until the barley is tender. Taste and adjust seasoning with salt and pepper if needed.

Serves 8 | PREP TIME: 10 minutes. COOK TIME: 50 minutes.

FIRE-ROASTED VEGETABLE SOUP

This is a family favorite during the summer. We grill a lot, and I make this soup with leftovers—it's a great way to make sure nothing is wasted and also very yummy and healthy for you, too!

Ingredients

2 large zucchini, halved

2 large yellow summer squash, halved

1 large red onion, cut into ½ inch slices

2 large carrots, quartered

1 large red pepper, halved

6 mushrooms, skewered

1 tbsp olive oil

½ tsp salt

½ tsp garlic powder

½ tsp oregano

¼ tsp freshly ground black pepper

1 shallot, minced

2 cloves garlic, minced

2 medium tomatoes, chopped

32 oz vegetable stock

½ cup acini di pepe pasta

1 tbsp butter

VEGAN FAVORITE

Cooking Instructions

Light a grill and rake the hot coals to one side. Spray or rub the zucchini, yellow squash, red onion, carrots, red pepper and mushrooms with the olive oil and then sprinkle with the spices. Grill the vegetables until just tender and a little bit charred on all sides, turning carefully as they cook, about 5-10 minutes. A grilling basket can be used if you prefer.

Once the vegetables are done remove to a plate and allow to cool. Sauté the minced shallot in a large stockpot set over medium heat until fragrant, about 5 minutes. Add the garlic to the pot and cook for one minute, stirring constantly. Add the chopped tomatoes and the stock to the pot and bring the soup to a simmer.

Now that the soup is simmering, chop the grilled vegetables into ½ inch chunks. Add them to the soup along with the acini di pepe pasta and cook until the pasta is al dente, about 6 minutes. Taste the soup and adjust seasonings as necessary with salt and pepper.

Serves 4-6 | PREP TIME: 10 minutes. COOK TIME: 45 minutes.

SEVEN-BEAN MÉLANGE

Mélange is French for mix and the combination of different beans gives this dish its unique flavor and texture. The recipe is easy to prepare, very hearty as well as being healthy for you. You can substitute different kinds of beans if desired or more convenient.

Ingredients

½ cup dry navy beans

½ cup dry pinto beans

½ cup dry chick peas

½ cup dry dark red kidney beans

½ cup dry Great Northern white beans

½ cup black-eyed peas

½ cup red lentils

1 medium red onion, diced

2 medium carrots, sliced

2 stalks celery, diced

2 cloves garlic, minced

1 tbsp tomato paste

½ tsp marjoram

¼ tsp thyme

½ tsp salt

¼ tsp freshly ground black pepper

32 oz vegetable stock

½ tsp liquid smoke (optional)*

½ tsp fresh parsley, chopped (for garnish)

Two sprigs of scallions chopped (for garnish)

Note: You'll need to soak the beans overnight.

Cooking Instructions

The night before you plan to make this soup, soak the dry beans in 1 gallon of water with 3 tbsp kosher salt. Before you cook, drain the beans, rinse well, then use as normal.

Sauté the onion, carrot and celery in a large stockpot set over medium heat until fragrant, about 5 minutes. Add the garlic, tomato paste, marjoram, thyme, salt, pepper and parsley to the pot and cook for 2 minutes, stirring constantly. Add the stock to the pot and bring the soup to a simmer. Once the soup reaches a simmer add all the beans and cook, partially covered, until the beans are tender, about 50-60 minutes. Stir in the liquid smoke and cook for another 5 minutes. Taste the soup and adjust seasonings as necessary with salt and pepper. Garnish with some fresh parsley and chopped scallions. I like to serve this with toasted pita bread.

Cook's Note:

Since this recipe was designed to be vegan, we use liquid smoke in this recipe to replicate the smoked bacon/ham element that is prevalent in most bean-soup recipes. Although it can be omitted it does add a nice depth of flavor to the dish.

VEGAN FAVORITE

Serves 6 | PREP TIME: 15 minutes. COOK TIME: 50-60 minutes.

HEARTY FRESH VEGETABLE

This is our first and oldest vegetable soup recipe, and the standard by which all newcomers are judged. It's a simple and easy recipe, one that does what it should; highlights the freshest vegetables in a simple yet flavorful broth. This recipe hasn't changed in 16 years for a reason.

Ingredients

1 medium yellow onion, diced

2 medium carrots, sliced

2 stalks celery, diced

2 cloves garlic, minced

2 tbsp tomato paste

½ tsp oregano

½ tsp salt

½ tsp parsley

¼ tsp freshly ground black pepper

2 tomatoes, peeled and chopped*

2 medium red skinned potatoes, diced

1 zucchini, quartered and sliced

8 oz or one cup of green beans, cut into 1 inch pieces

1 ear sweet corn, kernels cut from the cob

32 oz vegetable stock

VEGAN FAVORITE

Cooking Instructions

Sauté the onion, carrot and celery in a large stockpot set over medium heat until fragrant, about 5 minutes. Add the garlic, tomato paste, oregano, salt, pepper and parsley to the pot and cook for 2 minutes, stirring constantly. Add the tomatoes to the stock in the pot and bring the soup to a simmer. Once the soup reaches a simmer add the potatoes, zucchini and green beans and cook, covered, for 20 minutes or until the potatoes are tender. Remove from the heat and stir in the corn kernels. Taste the soup and adjust seasonings as necessary with salt and pepper. Garnish with some fresh parsley and serve with crusty sour dough rolls.

Cook's Note:

To easily peel the tomatoes, cut a cross on the bottom with a sharp knife and dunk them in boiling water for a minute, then dunk them in cold water. The skin should easily peel back.

Serves 4-6 | PREP TIME: 15 minutes. COOK TIME: 30 minutes.

CALIFORNIA VEGETABLE MEDLEY SOUP

This soup is great garnished with Cheese-it crackers! I know it sounds a little down market, but trust me. My family loves it that way.

Ingredients

1 medium onion, diced

1 carrot, diced

1 large red bell pepper, diced

2 stalks celery, diced

2 tbsp butter

2 cloves garlic, minced

1 tsp dried thyme

½ tsp dried marjoram

2 bay leaves

2 pinches red pepper flakes

32 oz vegetable stock

2 large zucchini, sliced

1 cup corn kernels, fresh or frozen

1 cup milk

12 oz or 1 ½ cups white cheddar cheese, grated

Cooking Instructions

Sauté the onion, carrots, red pepper and celery in the butter over medium-low heat in a large stockpot until translucent, about 8-10 minutes. Add the garlic and herbs, and cook for 1 minute while stirring. Add the vegetable stock and bring to a simmer. Cook for 10 minutes to allow the flavors to develop. Add the zucchini and corn, and cook until the zucchini is fork tender, about 10 minutes more. Then add the milk and turn heat to low. Add the cheese a couple ounces at a time and stir constantly until incorporated. Continue until all the cheese has been added. Taste and adjust seasonings with salt and pepper as needed.

Serves 6 | PREP TIME: 10 minutes. COOK TIME: 35 minutes.

MEDITERRANEAN VEGETABLE SOUP

This light and quick soup is especially good for lunch during the summer.

Ingredients

medium onion, diced
1 medium carrot, diced
1 medium red pepper, diced
8 oz fresh mushrooms, sliced
3 tbsp olive oil
2 cloves garlic, minced
½ tsp salt
½ tsp dried oregano
½ tsp dried rosemary
½ tsp dried winter savory
1 medium eggplant, peeled and cut into 1 inch chunks
1 yellow summer squash, sliced into half moons
32 oz vegetable stock
4 oz kalamata olives, pitted and sliced
1 can artichoke bottoms, sliced
2 bay leaves

Cooking Instructions

Sauté the onion, carrot, red pepper and mushrooms in the olive oil in a large stockpot set over medium heat until the onion is translucent, about 10 minutes. Add the garlic cloves, the salt and the dried herbs and cook for one minute, stirring constantly. Add the eggplant and squash to the pot and cook for 5 minutes to develop flavor. Increase the heat to medium high and add the vegetable stock. Once the soup comes to a simmer add the olives and the artichoke bottoms. Simmer the soup for 15 minutes to allow flavors to marry. Taste the soup and adjust seasonings with salt and pepper as needed.

We like to drizzle this soup with a bit of olive oil and serve it with some nice crusty bread on the side.

Serves 4 | PREP TIME: 15 minutes. COOK TIME: 35 minutes.

NORTH AFRICAN VEGETABLE SOUP

An adventurous yet simple recipe with ingredients that are easily found. This hearty vegan and gluten-free soup is easy to prepare and sure to satisfy. Garnish with chopped parsley and serve with wedges of toasted flatbread or pita.

Ingredients

1 large onion, chopped
2 carrots, sliced
1 tbsp olive oil
2 cloves garlic, minced
½ tsp salt
½ tsp cumin
½ tsp ground ginger
½ tsp tumeric
½ tsp harissa*
¼ tsp cinnamon
¼ tsp ground nutmeg
3 large tomatoes, chopped
32 oz vegetable stock
1 large sweet potato, peeled and cut into ½ inch chunks
2 small kohlrabis, peeled and cut into ½ inch chunks
2 parsnips, sliced

Cooking Instructions

Sauté the onion and the carrot in the olive oil in a large stockpot set over medium heat until fragrant, about 5 minutes. Add the garlic and spices to the pot and cook for two minutes, stirring constantly. Add the tomatoes and the stock to the pot and bring the soup to a simmer. Once a simmer is reached add the sweet potato, kohlrabi and parsnips. Cover and cook until the kohlrabi and yams are tender, about 30 minutes. Taste the soup and adjust seasonings as necessary with salt and pepper.

Cook's Note:

If you cannot find harissa (a North African chili powder spice blend) feel free to substitute ¼ tsp ground cayenne mixed with ¼ tsp ground coriander and a pinch of caraway seeds.

VEGAN FAVORITE

GLUTEN FREE

Serves 4 | PREP TIME: 10 minutes. COOK TIME: 40 minutes.

SWEET CORN CHOWDER

The most comfortable of comfort foods, thick and a great winter warmer.

Ingredients

4 medium red potatoes, washed and cut into ½ inch cubes

2 slices bacon

1 large onion, diced

2 tbsp butter

2 cloves garlic, minced

1 red bell pepper, diced

½ tsp red pepper flakes

1 tsp dried parsley

2 tbsp flour

16 oz whole milk

16 oz water

6 ears fresh sweet corn, husked and cut from the cob

Salt and pepper to taste

Cooking Instructions

Peel and cube the potatoes. Cook in a pan of boiling water for 10 minutes and then drain in a colander. While the potatoes are cooking, render the bacon over medium heat in a small skillet. When the bacon is finished, put it on paper towels to drain. Add the onion to the bacon drippings and cook for 5 minutes. Remove from heat.

Melt the butter in a stockpot over medium heat. Add the garlic and red pepper, and cook for 3 minutes, stirring constantly. Cut bacon into small pieces and add to the onions with the drippings. Add the red pepper flakes, the parsley and the flour and stir constantly for 5 minutes.

Add the milk, the water, the reserved potatoes and the corn. Heat the soup to a simmer and cook for another 20 minutes or until all the flavors have combined. Taste soup and adjust seasonings with salt or pepper.

Cook's Note:

Be sure to run the back of a knife down the cobs to extract all the corn and juice you can – there's LOTS of flavor in there!

Servings: 6 | PREP TIME: 15 minutes. COOK TIME: 35 minutes.

CUBAN BLACK BEAN SOUP

This simple and quick soup is vegan and gluten-free. The savory hint of cumin and chili powder balanced with the fresh cilantro and lime juice is a wonderful pairing.

Ingredients

1 medium onion, diced

1 medium carrot, diced

2 tbsp olive oil

½ tsp salt

2 cloves garlic, minced

2 large poblano peppers, roasted and chopped*

2 jalapeno peppers, roasted and chopped*

1 tsp cumin

½ tsp chili powder

2 cups dry black beans, soaked overnight in salted water

32 oz vegetable stock

Fresh cilantro leaves

Juice of two limes

Note: You'll need to soak the black beans overnight.

Cooking Instructions

Sauté the onion and carrot in the olive oil in a large stockpot set over medium heat until fragrant, about 5 minutes. Add the salt, garlic, roasted chiles and spices to the pot and cook for two minutes, stirring constantly. Add the beans and the stock to the pot and bring to a simmer. Cover the pot and cook until the beans are tender, about 30-40 minutes. Once the beans are tender, pulse soup in a food processor in batches to give the soup more body while leaving a lot of the beans whole. Taste the soup and adjust seasonings as necessary with salt and pepper. Garnish with fresh cilantro leaves and lime juice.

Cook's Note:

You can buy already roasted peppers in a jar. To roast the peppers in the oven, turn on the broiler, put the peppers on a broiler pan and place on the top shelf of the oven. Turn the peppers every fifteen minutes for an hour, then put in a bowl and cover with a towel to steam them a bit. Alternately you can roast them on the grill with the same approximate timing and finishing technique.

VEGAN FAVORITE

GLUTEN FREE

Serves 4 | PREP TIME: 10 minutes plus roasting of the peppers. COOK TIME: 45 minutes.

SPICY SOUTHWESTERN WHITE BEAN SOUP

This is another good example of a tasty, simple soup that is hearty and healthy, gluten-free and vegan. You'll be amazed at the amount of flavor packed into every bite. Garnish with scallions and serve with jalapeno corn bread and a cold beer. This is a satisfying end to a long day in the sun!

Ingredients

2 cups dry Great Northern white beans, soaked overnight in salted water

1 medium onion, diced

2 carrots, sliced

2 stalks celery, diced

2 tbsp olive oil

3 cloves garlic, minced

2 large poblano peppers, roasted and chopped*

1 serrano pepper, roasted and chopped*

1 bay leaf

½ tsp salt

½ tsp cumin

½ tsp chili powder

¼ tsp cayenne pepper

32 oz vegetable stock

Note: You'll need to soak the beans overnight.

Cooking Instructions

Sauté the onion, carrot and celery in the olive oil in a large stockpot set over medium heat until fragrant, about 5 minutes. Add the garlic, roasted chiles and all the spices to the pot and cook for two minutes, stirring constantly. Add the beans and stock to the pot and bring the soup to a simmer. Once a simmer is reached cover the pot and cook until the beans are tender, about 30-40 minutes. Once the beans are tender pulse in a food processor in batches to a thick but not quite smooth consistency. Taste the soup and adjust seasonings as necessary with salt and pepper.

Cook's Note:

As with the Cuban black-bean soup, you can buy already roasted peppers in a jar. To roast the peppers at home, turn on the broiler, put the peppers on a broiler pan and place on the top shelf of the oven. Turn the peppers every fifteen minutes for an hour, then put in a bowl and cover with a towel to steam them a bit. Alternately you can roast them on the grill with the same approximate timing and finishing technique. I often roast a few peppers while barbecuing other things to have them for these recipes.

Serves 4 | PREP TIME: 10 minutes plus roasting of the peppers (see below). COOK TIME: 45 minutes.

WEST INDIAN SQUASH SAMBAR

This recipe comes to us from a regular customer named Abshay. His mother made this recipe for his family all the time when he was little and he loved it. We started serving it at the store, and it got great reviews.

Ingrediants

1 acorn or Hubbard squash, roasted, peeled and cut into 1 inch chunks

1 large onion, diced

2 carrots, sliced

2 tbsp olive oil

2 cloves garlic, minced

1 tsp salt

½ tsp cumin

½ tsp red curry powder

½ tsp turmeric

½ tsp cayenne pepper

1 jalapeno pepper, seeded and diced

32 oz vegetable stock

1 cup red lentils

4 oz coconut milk

Salt and pepper to taste

Cooking Instructions

Roast the whole squash in a 400-degree oven for 30 minutes. Remove and allow to cool, then peel and chop the squash and set aside. Prepare the rest of the soup while the squash roasts.

Warm the oil in a stockpot over medium heat. Add the onion and carrot and sauté until softened, about 10 minutes. Add the garlic and the dry spices, and cook until fragrant, about one minute. Add the jalapeno pepper and the vegetable stock. Bring to a simmer and cook for 10 minutes. Add the lentils and the squash, and cook another 15 minutes to allow the lentils to soften and the flavors to develop. When the lentils and the squash are tender remove the soup from heat and add the coconut milk. Taste and add salt and pepper as needed.

VEGAN FAVORITE

GLUTEN FREE

Serves 6 | PREP TIME: 15 minutes. COOK TIME: 40-45 minutes.

WHITE BEAN & ESCAROLE SOUP

This is our take on a classic Italian recipe and one of my wife's favorites. She craves this in the middle of winter when fresh salad greens are out of season. Kale is a great substitute if you can't find escarole.

Ingredients

1 lb cannellini or Great Northern white beans, soaked overnight

4 oz pancetta or bacon, chopped

1 medium onion, diced

1 medium carrot, diced

1 stalk celery, diced

½ tsp dried oregano

¼ tsp dried marjoram

¼ tsp dried thyme

½ tsp salt

2 bay leaves

Pinch red pepper flakes

2 cloves garlic, minced

32 oz chicken or vegetable stock

1 head escarole, washed and cut into ribbons (tough stems removed)*

Salt and pepper to taste

Cooking Instructions

Cook the pancetta or bacon in a large stockpot over medium heat to render the fat, about 5 minutes. Add the onion, carrot and celery to the stockpot and cook over medium heat until translucent, about 10 minutes. Add the dried herbs, salt, pepper and garlic and cook for one minute, stirring constantly. Add the stock and the beans, and bring the soup to a simmer. Once the soup has reached a simmer cook for 20-30 minutes until the beans are tender, stirring occasionally. Once the beans are tender add the escarole and cook for another 15 minutes. Use the flat of a spatula to smash a few beans against the side of the stockpot to give the soup some extra body and a smoother texture. Taste the soup and adjust seasonings with salt and pepper as needed.

Cook's Note:

Escarole isn't available in many markets, so feel free to substitute kale or collard or mustard greens, all of which will taste great in this soup.

Serves 6 | PREP TIME: 15 minutes. COOK TIME: 30 minutes.

SPLIT-PEA SOUP

A traditional favorite inspired by my grandmother Bernadine's recipe.

Ingredients

16 oz dried split peas
2 tablespoons butter
1 cup onions diced
1 cup carrots diced
1 tablespoon minced garlic
16 oz smoked ham cut into half inch cubes
8 cups chicken stock
1 bay leaf
Salt and pepper to taste

Note: You'll need to soak the split peas for at least 8 hours ahead of time, or bring to a boil and let rest for an hour.

Cooking Instructions

Place the peas in a large pot or bowl, cover with water by 2 inches and soak 8 hours or overnight. Drain the peas and set aside. Alternately cover the peas with water and bring to a boil, then turn off the stove and let them rest for an hour before proceeding with the recipe.

In a large pot, melt the butter over medium-high heat. Add the onions and carrots and cook, stirring, for 5 minutes. Add the garlic and cook, stirring, for 1 minute. Add the ham and cook for another 5 minutes. Add the stock, the bay leaf, the drained peas and a pinch of salt and cook, stirring occasionally, until the peas are tender, about 1½ hours. Add more water as needed, if the soup becomes too thick or dry. Remove the bay leaf and discard. Season with salt and pepper to taste. Serve immediately.

Serves 8 | PREP TIME: 20 minutes. COOK TIME: 1½ hours.

YELLOW SPLIT-PEA SOUP WITH FENNEL

Yellow split peas have been with us since the times of the Roman Empire. This soup warms the soul and is the perfect accompaniment to a good book and your favorite blanket. Try it garnished with croutons or popcorn for a unique finish.

Ingredients

1 medium onion, diced

1 carrot, diced

2 stalks celery, diced

1 tbsp olive oil

2 cloves garlic, minced

1 small bulb of fennel, sliced (reserve the stalks and fronds for another use)

½ tsp salt

¼ tsp thyme

¼ tsp white pepper

1 lb yellow split peas, picked over to remove shriveled or broken peas, and rinsed

32 oz vegetable stock

Salt and pepper to taste

Cooking Instructions

Sauté the onion, carrots and celery in the olive oil in a large stockpot set over medium heat until fragrant, about 5 minutes. Add the garlic, fennel and spices to the pot and cook for two minutes, stirring constantly. Add the yellow spilt peas and the stock to the pot and bring the soup to a simmer. Once a simmer is reached, cover the pot, turn heat to low and cook until the split peas are just tender, about 30-40 minutes. Once the peas are tender pulse briefly with an immersion blender (or in batches in a food processor) to give the soup a bit more body and texture. Taste the soup and adjust seasonings as necessary with salt and pepper.

Serves 4-6 | PREP TIME: 15 minutes. COOK TIME: 45 minutes.

LIVELY LENTIL SOUP WITH LEMON

This is a quick and light soup that's great all year round. The contrast between the savory tomato paste and the creamy lentils is highlighted by a splash of lemon juice added at the end of cooking. Served with a nice salad, this recipe is a delicious and healthy lunch.

Ingredients

1 medium onion, diced

2 carrots, sliced

2 stalks celery, diced

1 tbsp olive oil

½ tsp salt

2 cloves garlic, minced

2 tbsp tomato paste

¼ tsp dried thyme

¼ tsp chervil

¼ tsp marjoram

2 tomatoes, chopped

1 lb green lentils, picked over to remove shriveled or broken lentils, and rinsed

32 oz vegetable stock

1 small zucchini, cut into half moons

Juice of two lemons

Salt and pepper to taste

Cooking Instructions

Sauté the onion, carrots and celery in the olive oil in a large stockpot set over medium heat until fragrant, about 5 minutes. Add the salt, garlic, the tomato paste and dried spices to the pot and cook for two minutes, stirring constantly. Add the tomatoes, lentils and the stock to the pot and bring the soup to a simmer. Cover the pot, and cook until the lentils are tender, about 20 minutes. Once the lentils are tender pulse briefly with an immersion blender (or take a small batch and pulse in a food processor and return to the soup) to give the soup a bit more body and texture. Add the zucchini and cook until just tender, about 5 minutes longer. Remove from the heat and stir in the lemon juice. Taste the soup and adjust seasonings as necessary with salt and pepper.

VEGAN FAVORITE

GLUTEN FREE

Serves 4-6 | PREP TIME: 10 minutes. COOK TIME: 30 minutes.

MASALA TOMATO LENTIL

Masala refers to a special spice paste with flavors from the Far East that we mix while the lentils cook. There are a lot of steps in the cooking process, but the rewards are evident in the bowl.

Ingredients

3 large tomatoes, halved

2 tbsp olive oil

3 cloves garlic, smashed

1 one inch piece of ginger, peeled and grated

1 tbsp garam masala spice blend

1 tsp red curry powder

½ tsp turmeric

¼ tsp cinnamon

¼ tsp cloves

½ tsp salt

½ tsp cumin

1 medium onion, diced

2 carrots, diced

2 stalks celery, diced

2 cups red lentils, picked over to remove shriveled and broken beans, and rinsed

32 oz vegetable stock

Salt and pepper to taste*

Cooking Instructions

Preheat the oven to 325 degrees. Drizzle the halved tomatoes with olive oil and sprinkle them with salt. Place them skin side down on a foil-lined baking sheet and roast in the oven for 90 minutes.

Make the masala spice paste and the rest of the soup while the tomatoes roast. Place the smashed cloves of garlic and the grated ginger in a mortar. Add the dry spices and mash everything together in the mortar until it becomes a rough paste. You should have about 1-2 tablespoons. Set aside.

Sauté the onion, carrot and celery in the remaining olive oil (about 1 tbsp) in a large stockpot set over medium heat until fragrant, about 5 minutes. Add the garlic and masala paste to the pot and cook for one minute, stirring constantly. Add the lentils and the stock to the pot and bring the soup to a simmer. Once a simmer is reached cover the pot and cook until the lentils are tender, about 20-25 minutes. When the tomatoes are done, pull them from the oven and add them to the soup. Pulse with an immersion blender (or pulse in your food processor in batches) to the desired consistency, making sure there are a few chunks left for texture. Taste the soup and adjust seasonings as necessary with salt and pepper.

VEGAN FAVORITE

GLUTEN FREE

Cook's Note:

Often times, especially when there are strong spices, home chefs under-salt their soups. This is fine if you want to reduce salt in your diet. But if you aren't going low sodium, and your soup isn't coming out perfectly, try adding ½ teaspoon salt or more.

Serves 4-6 | PREP TIME: 20 minutes. COOK TIME: 1 hour 45 minutes.

ROASTED CARROT & FENNEL SOUP

Fennel is a great counterpoint to the sweetness of carrots, making an appealing and balanced flavor combination to serve guests. If your significant other's parents are coming to dinner, this is the perfect soup to serve; It's complex and different but not difficult to make.

Ingredients

1 large bulb fennel, sliced (reserve some of the fronds for garnish)

6 large carrots, cut into 1 inch chunks

1 large onion, quartered

2 stalks celery, cut into 1 inch chunks

2 tbsp olive oil

1 tsp salt

½ tsp sugar

1 head of garlic, wrapped in foil

32 oz vegetable stock

1 tsp dried thyme

2 bay leaves

Salt and pepper to taste

Cooking Instructions

Preheat the oven to 375 degrees. Line a baking sheet with foil. Toss the fennel, carrots, onion and celery with the oil, salt and sugar, and place the vegetables on the baking sheet along with the head of garlic in foil. Roast in the oven for 30-40 minutes until soft, turning the vegetables a couple times so they cook evenly. While the vegetables roast, add the stock and the dried herbs to a large pot and keep warm on low heat. Once the vegetables are browned and soft, remove from the oven and add them to the warmed stock. Remove the bay leaves and purée the soup with an immersion blender (or food processor in batches) until the soup is thick and almost smooth. Taste and adjust seasonings with salt and pepper as needed.

VEGAN FAVORITE

GLUTEN FREE

Serves 6 | PREP TIME: 10 minutes. COOK TIME: 45 minutes.

PEARL'S BIRTHDAY SOUP

We first discovered the Little Bear series* of books when my daughter Pearl was 3 years old. These books quickly became her favorite for our nightly reading before bed, and her very favorite story was the one in which Little Bear wakes up on his birthday to find his mother isn't home and there's no cake. So Little Bear takes it upon himself to make birthday soup for himself and all his friends with carrots and potatoes, peas and tomatoes. We were so inspired that we made our own version to serve at the store.

Ingredients

4 medium carrots, sliced

2 stalks celery, small diced

1 small onion, small diced

1 clove garlic, minced

2 bay leaves

1 tsp dried thyme

1 tsp dried parsley

½ tsp dried marjoram

32 oz vegetable stock

3 fresh tomatoes, diced (or one 14.5 ounce canned diced tomatoes)

½ tsp salt

1 cup fresh or frozen peas

2 large potatoes, medium diced

6 oz rotini pasta

Salt and pepper to taste

Cooking Instructions

Sauté the carrots, celery and onion in a stockpot over medium heat until translucent; about 10 minutes. Add the garlic and the dried herbs and cook for one minute. Add the vegetable stock, the tomatoes and the salt and bring to a simmer, stirring occasionally. Once the soup has reached a simmer, add the peas, potatoes and pasta, and cook until tender, approximately 20 minutes. Taste the soup and adjust seasonings with salt and pepper as needed.

Cook's Note:

Pearl likes potatoes and noodles in her soup. The rotini can be omitted easily enough to make this gluten-free. Just add another potato to maintain the heartiness of the dish.

*(by Else Holmelund Minarik and Maurice Sendak)

VEGAN FAVORITE

GLUTEN FREE*

*Can be made gluten free by omitting the pasta and adding another potato.

Serves 6 | PREP TIME. 10 minutes. COOK TIME: 35 minutes.

ROASTED CARROT & GINGER BISQUE

Roasting the vegetables brings out the natural sugars while the ginger adds a touch of heat for a nice flavor twist. This soup is versatile enough to stand as an entrée or a lunch, and is easy to make. It's a mainstay first course at our house for dinner parties.

Ingredients

1 lb carrots, cut into chunks
1 large sweet potato, peeled and quartered
1 medium onion, quartered
1 clove garlic, smashed
32 oz vegetable stock
1 tbsp grated fresh ginger
1 tbsp olive oil
1 bay leaf
½ tsp salt
½ tsp granulated sugar
¼ tsp white pepper

Cooking Instructions

Preheat the oven to 400 degrees. Toss the carrots, sweet potato and onion with the salt and the sugar in the olive oil and turn out onto a foil lined baking sheet. Roast uncovered in the oven for 20 minutes or until caramelized. Remove from the oven and add the vegetables and vegetable stock to a large pot set over medium heat. Add the ginger, garlic and white pepper and bring the soup to a simmer. Once a simmer is reached turn the heat to low and cook for 10 minutes until the flavors marry. Remove from the heat and pulse with an immersion blender to desired consistency. Taste the soup and adjust seasonings as necessary with salt and pepper. Garnish with fresh parsley.

VEGAN FAVORITE

GLUTEN FREE

Serves 4 | PREP TIME: 10 minutes. COOK TIME: 35 minutes

SAVORY CREAM OF ASPARAGUS

One of spring's first vegetables to appear, asparagus is great on the grill and in salads, but also shines in a soup like this. We planted asparagus in our community garden plot six years ago. At first, yields were low, but once the asparagus plants established themselves, they really took off. So much so that there was far too much for us to grill, blanch or put into other dishes, so I came up with this recipe. It's quick to make and freezes well, which makes homegrown asparagus a year-round pleasure.

Ingredients

4 tbsp butter

2 shallots, diced

3 tbsp flour

1 clove garlic, minced

½ tsp salt

¼ tsp black pepper

16 oz vegetable or chicken stock

16 oz milk

1 lb asparagus, washed and cut into 1 inch pieces

1 cup heavy cream

Salt and pepper to taste

Cooking Instructions

Melt the butter in a large stockpot over medium heat. Sauté the shallots in the butter until fragrant, about 5 minutes. Add the flour and cook for 3 minutes, stirring constantly. Add the garlic, salt and pepper to the pot and cook for 2 minutes more, stirring constantly. Add the stock and the milk, and bring to a slow simmer, stirring regularly. The soup will finish thickening shortly after a simmer is reached, about 10 minutes. Add the asparagus pieces and cook until tender, about 10 minutes longer. Once the asparagus is tender, you can remove some of the pieces to use to garnish. Pulse the soup with an immersion blender (or food processor in batches) until smooth. Return the purée to the pot, remove from heat and stir in the heavy cream. Taste the soup and adjust seasonings as necessary with salt and pepper. Garnish with reserved asparagus pieces and serve.

Serves 4 | PREP TIME: 15 minutes. COOK TIME: 30 minutes

FRESH TOMATO & BASIL BISQUE

Our take on a classic tomato soup. It's a homerun with the roasted tomatoes combined with the light garlic flavor.

Ingredients

1 medium onion, ¼ inch diced

2 medium carrots, ¼ inch diced

2 tbsp butter

2 cloves garlic, minced

2 lbs fresh tomatoes, peeled and seeded (we use Roma tomatoes)

24 oz vegetable stock

1 cup heavy cream

1 cup fresh basil leaves, cut into chiffonade (long thin strips done by folding the leaves or rolling them before cutting them)

Salt and fresh ground pepper to taste

GLUTEN FREE

Cooking Instructions

Sauté the onion and carrots in the butter over medium heat in a large stockpot until translucent, about 10 minutes. Add the garlic and cook two minutes longer. Add the tomatoes and cook for 10 minutes, breaking them up with a spatula as they cook. Add the vegetable stock and bring the soup to a simmer. Simmer for 5 minutes to allow the flavors to marry. Remove the soup from the heat and process with an immersion blender (or food processor in batches) until smooth. Add the heavy cream and basil leaves. Taste and adjust seasonings as needed with salt and pepper.

Cook's Note:

I like to garnish this with a spoonful of mascarpone cheese right before I serve it.

Serves 6 | PREP TIME: 15 minutes. COOK TIME: 40–45 minutes.

SUN-DRIED TOMATO & ROASTED GARLIC SOUP

This soup is like the Tomato Basil Bisque's sophisticated cousin.
The sun-dried tomatoes add deeper flavor to the dish.

Ingredients

1 medium onion, diced
1 medium carrot, diced
1 stalk celery, diced
2 tbsp olive oil
2 bay leaves
½ tsp dried oregano
½ tsp dried basil
½ tsp salt
¼ tsp white pepper
1 head garlic, roasted and mashed (divided)
32 oz chicken stock
2 lbs fresh tomatoes, peeled seeded and diced
6 oz sun dried tomatoes, chopped
1 cup heavy cream
Salt and pepper to taste

Cooking Instructions

Sauté the onion, carrot and celery in the olive oil in a large stockpot over medium heat until translucent, about 10 minutes. Add the dried herbs, salt, pepper and half of the roasted garlic and cook for one minute, stirring constantly. Add the chicken stock and the fresh tomatoes and bring the soup to a simmer. Once the soup has reached a simmer, cook for another 15 minutes to allow the flavor to develop. Purée the soup with an immersion blender until smooth. Add the sun-dried tomatoes and the rest of the mashed garlic, and remove from the heat. Stir in the heavy cream. Taste the soup and adjust seasonings with salt and pepper as needed.

GLUTEN
FREE

Serves 6 | PREP TIME: 10 minutes. COOK TIME: 50 minutes.

TOMATO FLORENTINE SOUP

When I think of Tomato Florentine Soup, I think of being nervous. I made this for the host on Fox during my first time on TV because it's easy to make and a heartier soup that eats like a meal. I was so nervous, I kept calling the hostess "ma'am," and the young, thin woman was getting annoyed. I thought I'd blown it for me and the restaurant, but since then I've made numerous TV appearances, and can look back and laugh at the learning experience. Anyway, this is a great soup, which is why I picked it, sir.

Ingrediants

12 oz uncooked sweet Italian sausage, crumbled

1 medium onion, small dice

1 stalk celery, small dice

1 medium carrot, small dice

2 tablespoons olive oil

2 cloves garlic, minced

4 cups fresh tomatoes or 2 (14.5 ounce) cans diced tomatoes

1 (14.5 ounce) can tomato sauce

32 oz homemade stock or canned beef broth

1 tsp dried basil

1 tsp dried thyme

1 tsp dried oregano

2 bay leaves

1 bunch fresh spinach, washed & chopped or one box frozen chopped spinach thawed and drained

1 cup pasta shells

Salt and pepper to taste

Cooking Instructions

Warm a saucepan over medium heat. Add 1 tablespoon of the oil and cook the sausage, onion, celery and carrot over medium heat until the meat is no longer pink. Drain. Stir in the other tablespoon of oil, the garlic, tomatoes, stock, tomato sauce, basil, thyme, oregano and bay leaves. Bring to a boil. Reduce heat; cover and simmer for 10 minutes. Add the spinach and the pasta shells and cook for another 10-15 minutes to allow the shells to cook and the flavors to meld. Taste the soup and adjust with salt and pepper as needed. Serve immediately.

Cook's Note:

To roast the garlic, preheat the oven to 400 degrees. Peel away the outer layer of the garlic's skin. Cut the top off the whole clove of garlic so each individual clove is cut. Pour a teaspoon of oil over the clove (or cloves if you want to cook more and save some for other uses). Put the clove or cloves on a baking sheet and cover with aluminum foil. Roast for 30 minutes. The cloves should be browned and soft all the way through. When cool, use a small fork to remove the cloves or squeeze each one out. Mmmmm, good in this soup, on toast or both!

Serves 4 | PREP TIME: 20 minutes. COOK TIME: 45 minutes.

CLASSIC MULLIGATAWNY

The name of this fantastic British and Indian creation means 'pepper water.'

Ingredients

1 large red onion, diced
2 stalks of celery, diced (leaves included)
1 carrot, diced
1 tbsp olive oil
1 tbsp butter
1 lb chicken breast, cubed
2 cloves garlic, minced
½ tsp salt
1 tbsp curry powder
½ tsp cumin
¼ tsp cinnamon
¼ tsp clove
¼ tsp turmeric
¼ tsp white pepper
32 oz chicken stock
1 cup red lentils
1 granny smith apple, peeled, cored and diced
½ cup heavy cream
Salt and pepper to taste
Fresh cilantro for garnish

Cooking Instructions

Melt the butter with the olive oil in a large stockpot over medium hot. Sauté the onion, celery and carrot in the olive oil until translucent, about 8 minutes. Add the chicken and cook until done, about 10 minutes. Add the garlic, salt, curry powder, cumin, cinnamon, clove, turmeric and white pepper to the pot and cook for two minutes, stirring constantly. Add the stock, lentils and diced apple to the pot and bring to a simmer. Once the soup reaches a simmer cover the pot, turn heat to low and cook for 20 minutes until the lentils are done. Taste and adjust seasonings as necessary with salt and pepper. Remove from heat and stir in the heavy cream. Garnish with fresh cilantro. This goes well served with rice but can be eaten on its own, too.

GLUTEN FREE

Serves 4-6 | PREP TIME: 10 minutes. COOK TIME: 20 minutes.

STUFFED GREEN PEPPER SOUP

This soup came together because I was trying to be thrifty and assemble leftovers I had around and the soup turned out really tasty and with a little different flavor so I worked on this for the shops. Soup is the best way to reinvent leftovers.

Ingredients

1 lb ground sirloin

2 large green peppers, chopped

2 cloves garlic, minced

3 fresh roma tomatoes, seeded and chopped or one 14.5 oz can diced tomatoes

1 small onion, small dice

1 stalk celery, small dice

48 oz beef stock

2 oz tomato paste

1 tsp dried thyme

½ tsp freshly ground black pepper

2 tbsp soy sauce

1 tbsp brown sugar

1 cup white or basmati rice

Salt and pepper to taste

Cooking Instructions

Brown the ground beef with the onion and celery in a large stockpot over medium heat. Drain well. Add the green peppers, garlic and tomatoes and return to heat. Add the onion and cook on medium heat for 5 minutes to allow flavors to develop. Add the beef stock, tomato paste, thyme, pepper, soy sauce and the brown sugar and bring soup to a simmer. Once the soup reaches a simmer add the rice and cook till the rice is done, about 20 minutes. Taste the soup and adjust seasonings with salt and pepper as needed.

Serves 4 | PREP TIME: 20 minutes. COOK TIME: 35 minutes.

BROCCOLI RABE SOUP WITH LENTILS & SPRING ONIONS

Broccoli rabe (also known as rapini) is a wild form of the traditional broccoli we know and love. It forms smaller heads than regular broccoli, but the stems and leaves can also be used and are delicious. Here the broccoli rabe is nicely paired with earthy lentils and spring onions. This simple soup is a joy to serve and eat.

Ingredients

3 spring onions, diced (you can substitute any other sweet onion)

2 carrots, chopped

2 stalks celery, sliced

2 tbsp butter

1 lb broccoli rabe, washed and cut into 1-inch lengths (leaves included)

2 cloves garlic, minced

1 pinch red pepper flakes

1 tsp thyme

½ tsp marjoram

1 bay leaf

1 cup green lentils, rinsed and picked over

1 tbsp tomato paste

48 oz vegetable stock

1 tsp lemon zest, minced

Cooking Instructions

Set a 4-quart stockpot on high heat with one inch of water and a steamer basket set inside. Sauté the onion, carrots and celery in the butter over medium low heat in another large stockpot until translucent, about 8-10 minutes.

While the aromatics are cooking, steam the broccoli rabe for 10 minutes.

Add the garlic, the pepper flakes and the herbs to the pot with the aromatics. Cook for 1 minute, stirring constantly. Add the lentils, tomato paste and vegetable stock. Bring to a simmer, cover and turn heat to low. Cook for 20-25 minutes until the lentils are soft and the flavors have developed. Add the lemon zest. Taste and adjust seasonings with salt and pepper as needed.

Cook's Note:

Spring onions are onions picked before they get a chance to form bulbs. Normally they are a bit sweeter than regular onions. They can be found in farmers' markets in May and June. Also, steaming the broccoli rabe before adding it to the soup (rather than just dropping it into the soup) is a good idea because of this vegetable's strong taste— it's a bitter green after all. Steaming takes out some of the bitterness and gives it a nice mellow flavor.

Serves 6 | PREP TIME: 10 minutes. COOK TIME: 25 minutes.

SUMMER'S BOUNTY GREEN BEAN & ZUCCHINI SOUP WITH QUINOA

This soup takes advantage of the late-July green beans and zucchini harvest in our garden. It's easy, freezes well and is delicious. The bacon and farm-fresh vegetables are an unbeatable combination. Add tasty quinoa, one of the few vegetables that contains all nine of the essential amino acids for your body, and it's healthy to boot, a win-win in my book. I like to serve this soup with hearty toasted pumpernickel bread.

Ingredients

4 oz bacon, cut into ½ inch squares
1 medium yellow onion, diced
2 medium carrots, sliced
2 stalks celery, diced
1 tbsp canola oil
2 cloves garlic, minced
2 tbsp tomato paste
½ tsp dried thyme
½ tsp salt
½ tsp freshly ground black pepper
½ tsp dried parsley
2 tomatoes, peeled and chopped
32 oz vegetable stock
12 oz green beans, cut into 1-inch pieces
2 zucchinis, quartered and sliced in ¼ inch pieces
1 cup quinoa
Salt and pepper to taste
Parsley, chopped for garnish

Cooking Instructions

Sauté the bacon with the onion, carrot and celery in the canola oil in a large stockpot set over medium heat until fragrant, about 5 minutes. Add the garlic, tomato paste, thyme, salt, pepper and parsley, and cook for one minute, stirring constantly. Add the tomatoes and stock. Bring to a simmer and add the green beans, zucchini and quinoa. Cover and cook for 20 minutes until the beans are tender and the quinoa is done. Taste the soup and adjust seasonings as necessary with salt and pepper. Garnish with fresh parsley.

GLUTEN
FREE

Serves 6 | PREP TIME: 15 minutes. COOK TIME: 30 minutes.

WINTER VEGETABLE SOUP

This recipe is relatively new for us. I learned only a year or two ago that many vegetables can be successfully cultivated right up to the arrival of snow in Chicago, and some, like leeks and kale can take the cold weather quite well. This hearty and satisfying soup is perfect for an early winter bounty. If there ever was a soup that went perfectly in a sourdough bread bowl, this is this one.

Ingredients

1 large onion, diced
2 carrots, sliced
2 stalks celery, sliced
2 tbsp canola oil
2 garlic cloves, minced
1 tsp dried thyme
1 tsp salt
1 tsp black pepper
1 tsp dried rosemary
1 tsp dried marjoram
1 tsp dried parsley
48 oz vegetable stock
1 small bulb of fennel, sliced
2 parsnips, sliced
2 medium turnips, peeled and diced
2 medium red potatoes, peeled and diced
1 bunch of kale, stemmed and cut into strips
Salt and pepper to taste
Fresh parsley, chopped for garnish
Parmesan shavings for garnish

Cooking Instructions

Sauté the onion, carrot and celery in the canola oil in a large stockpot set over medium heat until fragrant, about 5 minutes. Add the garlic, thyme, salt, pepper, rosemary, marjoram and parsley and cook for one minute, stirring constantly. Add the stock and bring to a simmer. Add the fennel, parsnips, turnips, potatoes and kale. Cover and cook for 30-40 minutes or until the parsnip and potatoes are tender. Taste the soup and adjust seasonings as necessary with salt and pepper. Garnish with fresh parsley and some shavings of parmesan if desired.

VEGAN FAVORITE

GLUTEN FREE

Serves 6 | PREP TIME: 15 minutes. COOK TIME: 45 minutes.

CHAPTER TWO

SAUSAGE, BACON, BEEF AND OTHER MEATY FLAVORS

From age 17 to 22 I was a vegetarian. I had a vegetarian girlfriend I was in love with. I was also turned off by people taking meat for granted. I didn't feel people appreciated how big a deal it was to kill a cow. My first post-vegetarian meal was a steak. It was fantastic, and I ate the whole thing. I now eat meat and love it, but also try to remember my farming and idealistic roots, and appreciate the animals we eat. When you make our soups (or for any meal, really), I recommend you pick your meat carefully and buy from butchers you like and trust.

To make great meaty soups, take your time. Meat doesn't like to be rushed, or moved around. Browning the meat properly is important to the flavor. Heat the pot as hot as you can without the oil smoking, place the meat in carefully. It's important that you brown meat in small batches with room in the pot; too much meat will cool the pan down too fast, and the meat will release liquid and steam. So be patient and brown the meat in a few batches. Let it sizzle in the oil rather than moving it around so you get nice, flavorful, dark-brown spots. Patience is the key to great-tasting meaty soups.

BERNADINE'S SMOKED HAM WITH GREAT NORTHERN WHITE BEANS

My grandmother Bernadine would make this soup on dark, cold winter days. I remember seeing the beans soaking in a bowl of water one night and sitting down to eat big bowls of this the next day. The smoked ham hock adds a lot of flavor and body to the soup, but if you're looking for a lighter flavor, use a leaner smoked ham steak instead. Bernadine served this with cornbread made in a cast-iron pan, but I've also had it with croutons and loved it that way too.

Excellent!

Ingredients

1 lb dried Great Northern white beans

1 large red onion, chopped

1 carrot, sliced

2 stalks celery, sliced

2 tbsp butter

2 cloves garlic, minced

½ tsp salt

1 bay leaf

¼ tsp black pepper

¼ tsp thyme

64 oz chicken stock

1 smoked ham hock (about 1 lb)

Fresh parsley for garnish

Salt and pepper to taste

Note: You'll need to soak the beans overnight.

Cooking Instructions

Soak the beans in enough water to cover overnight. Add a pinch of salt to the water.

Melt the butter in a large pan over medium heat. Sauté the onion, carrot and celery in the butter until fragrant, about 5 minutes. Add the garlic, salt, bay leaf, pepper and thyme to the pot and cook for 2 minutes, stirring constantly. Add the stock, ham hock and the drained white beans to the pot and bring to a simmer. Then partly cover and cook until the beans are done, about 1 hour, stirring occasionally. Add more stock if the soup becomes too thick. Taste the soup and adjust seasonings as needed with salt and pepper. Garnish with fresh parsley and serve.

Used great Northern Beans, did the quicksoak method per directions on dried bean bag

GLUTEN FREE

Serves 4 | PREP TIME: 10 minutes. COOK TIME: 1 hour 15 minutes.

SPICY LENTIL AND LAMB SAUSAGE STEW

The spices intermixed with the lamb sausage provide a complex backdrop for the sweet carrot and salty green lentils in this dish. Served with a nice loaf of crusty bread and a glass of good wine, this makes a beautiful dinner out of simple ingredients.

Ingredients

1 medium onion, diced

2 carrots, cut into half moons

2 stalks of celery, diced

½ tsp salt

2 tbsp butter

1 lb lamb Merguez sausage, cut into ½ inch chunks

2 cloves garlic, minced

2 bay leaves

1 tsp red pepper flakes

½ tsp dried thyme

½ tsp dried oregano

¼ tsp dried rosemary

24 to 48 oz chicken stock, as needed

2 cups dry green lentils

Salt and pepper to taste

Cooking Instructions

Melt the butter over medium low heat in a large stockpot. Add the onion, carrots, celery and salt, and sauté until fragrant, about 5 minutes. Add the sausage, garlic and all the spices, and cook for 2 minutes, stirring constantly. Add half the chicken stock and all the lentils, and bring to a simmer. Cover and turn heat to low. Cook until the lentils are tender, about 30-40 minutes, stirring occasionally. Then taste soup and adjust seasonings as needed with salt and pepper. Stew may also be thinned to the desired consistency with extra stock at this point; if you'd prefer a thick stew omit adding more stock.

Note to self
Do sausage 1st + scrape up
brown bits - then add mirapeux

GLUTEN FREE

Serves 6-8 | PREP TIME: 15 minutes. COOK TIME: 45 minutes.

BACON, TOMATO & CHEDDAR CHOWDER

Sounds odd on the page but tastes great in the spoon. This simple rustic chowder can be thrown together on a moment's notice and will delight whoever is around to share in it. I like to garnish this with fresh parsley and serve it with toasted multigrain rolls and a simple romaine salad.

Ingredients

1 lb thick-cut bacon, cut into one-inch squares
2 shallots, diced
1 carrot, diced
1 stalk celery, diced
1 tbsp canola oil
2 cloves garlic, minced
½ tsp salt
¼ tsp black pepper
1 tbsp flour
¼ tsp thyme
32 oz chicken stock
3 large tomatoes, chopped
1 large potato, peeled and diced
8 oz sharp cheddar cheese, shredded
Fresh parsley for garnish
Salt and pepper to taste

Cooking Instructions

Warm a large pot over medium-low heat and add the bacon. Cook over medium low until the fat renders, about 10 minutes. Be careful not to turn the heat up, or you'll burn the bacon (see note below). Once the bacon is done remove it to a plate. Add the canola oil to the pot and raise the heat to medium high. Sauté the shallots, carrot and celery over medium heat until fragrant, about 5 minutes. Add the garlic, salt, pepper, flour and thyme to the pot, and cook for 2 minutes, stirring constantly. Add the stock and the tomatoes, and bring to a simmer. Once a simmer is reached, add the bacon and potatoes to the pot, and cook until the potatoes are tender, about 15 minutes. Taste the soup and adjust seasonings as needed with salt and pepper. Remove from the heat and stir in the cheese about 4 ounces at a time. Garnish with fresh parsley and serve.

Cook's Note

The potato is there for two reasons, 1. all chowders have potato, and it can't be chowder without potato and 2. the tater breaks down with cooking and lends extra body to the chowder. The key to the flavor here, however, is to cook the bacon slowly. That way you only render the fat instead of burning any of the proteins.

Serves 4 | PREP TIME: 10 minutes. COOK TIME: 25 minutes

BAYOU CHICKEN & SAUSAGE GUMBO

This is our version of the New Orleans tradition. There are many variations of gumbo and ours is an accessible entry into the world of Cajun foods.

Ingredients

1 chicken, cut into 8 pieces
1 tsp paprika
1 tsp seasoned salt
½ tsp white pepper
½ cup canola oil
½ cup flour
1 large onion, diced
1 green pepper, diced
2 stalks celery, diced
1 lb Andouille sausage, cut into ½ inch chunks
5 cloves of garlic, smashed
½ tsp thyme
½ tsp salt
64 oz chicken stock
1 cup long grain white rice
1 cup frozen okra, thawed
½ tsp cayenne pepper, or to taste
1 tsp filé powder

Cooking Instructions

Mix the paprika, seasoned salt and white pepper, and sprinkle liberally over the chicken. Warm the oil in a large stockpot over medium-high heat. Brown the chicken in the hot oil, about 4 minutes per side. Remove and set aside. Lower heat to medium low and add the flour. Stir constantly with a wooden spatula to avoid burning for 15-20 minutes until a light caramel color is achieved; this is the roux that thickens the gumbo. Add the onion, pepper and celery, and cook until translucent, about 10 minutes. Add the sausage, garlic, thyme and salt, and cook for two minutes, stirring constantly. Add the reserved chicken pieces along with the chicken stock and bring the gumbo to a boil. Then turn the heat to medium low and simmer the gumbo for one hour. After an hour, remove the chicken, allow to cool and pull the meat from the bones. Add the rice directly to the pot and simmer until the rice is tender, about 20 – 25 minutes. Stir in the pulled chicken, the okra and the cayenne pepper to taste and cook for another 15 minutes to allow the flavors to develop. Remove from the heat and stir in the filé powder. Serve in deep bowls garnished with scallions.

Cook's Note:

There is 'creole' gumbo and then there's 'cajun' gumbo. Creole is the New Orleans French-Quarter style seafood gumbo, while Cajun gumbo uses more fowl and game meats, along with more peppers and heat. Filé powder is made from sassafras leaves and give gumbo its distinctive flavor. In our recipe we cut the normal amount of okra and add only a touch of filé powder right at the end of cooking so that you can taste it but it's not overpowering.

Serves 8 | PREP TIME: 25 minutes. COOK TIME: 2 hours.

ITALIAN WEDDING SOUP

The stories behind this soup are all over the map. The one that makes the most sense to me, though its veracity is unverified, goes as follows; this soup was served at traditional Italian weddings because the shape of the meatballs were symbolic of a well-rounded marriage for the newlyweds. It's a nice thought and a great meal to boot.

Ingredients

16 oz ground beef (we use sirloin)
2 eggs, beaten
¼ cup dried bread crumbs
¼ cup grated Parmesan cheese
½ teaspoon basil
½ teaspoon oregano
½ teaspoon thyme

1 medium onion, diced
2 medium carrots, diced
1 stalk celery, diced
1 tablespoon olive oil
2 cloves garlic, minced
32 oz chicken broth
1 bay leaf
2 cups spinach, washed, trimmed and sliced
1 cup acini de pepe pasta
Salt and pepper to taste

Cooking Instructions

Place the beef in a medium sized mixing bowl. Add the egg, bread crumbs, cheese, basil, oregano and thyme. Shape mixture into 1 inch round balls. Set meatballs aside.*

Add the olive oil to a large stockpot over medium heat. Add the onion, carrots and celery, and cook for 5 minutes. Add the garlic, chicken broth and bay leaf, and bring to a simmer. Stir in the spinach and meatballs. Allow the soup to return to a simmer; then reduce heat to medium low. Be careful not to let the soup reach a rolling boil, which could toughen the meatballs. A slow gentle poach will give you good, tender meatballs. Cook, stirring frequently, until the meatballs are no longer pink inside, about 10 minutes. Stir in the pasta and cook for an additional 5 minutes until the pasta is done.

Cook's Note:

When packing the meatballs, do it gently, and pack the meat in your hands just tightly enough to hold together when dropped into the simmering water. Try not to squeeze or knead the meat, which can make it tough.

Serves 6 | PREP TIME: 15 minutes. COOK TIME: 25 minutes.

PIZZA LOVERS' SOUP

Yes, you read it right. Everything you love in a pizza but in soup form. A friend challenged me to make this for a charity event. The reactions were great so we added it to our lineup. It never sold all that well, but those who loved it would buy it by the gallon. It's important to note the ingredients for this soup are perhaps the most malleable of all these recipes; not everyone likes black olives or spinach on their pizza after all. Serve this with plenty of cheesy garlic bread and a pitcher of cola. Is that Miss Pacman music I hear in the background?

Ingredients

1 small yellow onion, sliced
1 medium green pepper, sliced
1 tbsp butter
2 cloves garlic, minced
½ tsp salt
¼ tsp basil
¼ tsp oregano
¼ tsp crushed red chili flakes
2 tbsp tomato paste
8 oz fresh spinach, washed and trimmed
24 oz beef stock
12 oz can tomato sauce
3 medium tomatoes, chopped
8 oz pepperoni
8 oz cooked Italian sausage, crumbled
4 oz sliced black olives
Salt and pepper to taste
Fresh basil and grated parmesan cheese for garnish

GLUTEN FREE

Cooking Instructions

Sauté the onion and green pepper in the butter until fragrant in a large stockpot set over medium heat, about 5 minutes. Add the garlic, salt, basil, oregano, chili flakes, tomato paste and spinach to the pot, and cook for two minutes, stirring constantly. Add the stock, tomato sauce and chopped tomatoes to the pot, and bring to a simmer. Then add the pepperoni and the sausage. Cover the pot, turn the heat to low and continue cooking for another 15 minutes to allow the flavors to develop. Add the black olives and warm through, about 5 minutes. Taste and adjust seasonings as necessary with salt and pepper. Ladle into bowls and garnish with fresh basil and the grated parmesan.

Cook's Note:

Unique and odd, this soup is something a lot of people ask about and/or try while at the store, and then ultimately leave with something else. It deserves a spot in the rotation as a 'buzz generator.' We have several other soups like this; they don't sell well but nearly everyone asks about them at the door or tries them before moving on to what they walked in to get. In that respect this is a very popular soup even though sales records indicate otherwise. It's a conversation starter.

Serves 4 – 6 | PREP TIME: 10 minutes. COOK TIME: 25 minutes.

SICHUAN BEEF NOODLE SOUP

This is a broth-based beefy noodle stew, the kind your spice-loving Chinese neighbor would make for you because she heard you had a cold—which is how I first had this soup. It takes time to make and some ingredients are hard to source but it's worth it because this soup packs a powerful wallop of flavor and texture. It's a delicious way to clear your head or warm up after shoveling the driveway.

Ingredients

1 large Vidalia onion, chopped

4 oz shitake mushrooms, sliced

2 carrots, sliced

1 head bok choy, washed, trimmed and chopped (leaves included)

2 tbsp canola oil

3 cloves garlic, minced

1 tbsp soy sauce

1 tbsp brown sugar

1 tbsp chili paste

1 1-inch piece of ginger, peeled and diced

½ tsp salt

½ tsp Sichuan peppercorns

1 lime, halved

2 lbs meaty beef shanks

1 small daikon radish, peeled and cut into ¼ inch half moons

48 oz beef stock

1 lb thick wheat noodles (cho mein)

Fresh cilantro, chopped for garnish

Salt and pepper to taste

Serve with soy sauce and chili paste as condiments

Cooking Instructions

Put 2 quarts of water into a large stockpot and set it on the stove, covered. Reserve to cook the noodles when you are ready.

Heat the canola oil in another large stockpot set over high heat. Sauté the onion, mushrooms, carrot, and bok choy until fragrant, about 5 minutes. Add the garlic, soy sauce, brown sugar, chili paste, ginger, salt, peppercorns and lime to the pot and cook for two minutes, stirring constantly. Add the beef shanks, daikon radish and stock to the pot, and bring the soup to a simmer. Then cover the pot and turn the heat to low. Continue cooking until the beef shanks are tender and nearly falling apart, 1 to 1½ hours. Remove beef and set aside to cool.

Start the other stockpot with the water and cook the noodles according to package directions.

While the noodles cook, separate the beef from the bones, removing any fat. Cut the beef into bite-sized pieces and add it back to the stew. Taste the stew and adjust as necessary with salt and pepper. Ladle the noodles into large bowls and top with a couple generous ladles of stew. Garnish with fresh cilantro and serve with soy sauce and chili paste on the side.

Cook's Note:

I make this or pho when my wife Kris, or I come down with a cold. Pertinent medicine she calls it. Sometimes I'll just let things simmer all day; the smells that come out are as good for you as the stew.

Serves 4 – 6 | PREP TIME: 20 minutes. COOK TIME: 2 hours.

ALBONDIGAS OR MEXICAN MEATBALL SOUP

Spicy meatballs are poached in a flavorful broth for a soup that eats like a meal. I had this soup for the first time in Mexico on our honeymoon. I liked it so much, I had it for lunch every day for the next three days.

Ingredients

1 lb ground beef (I recommend 85% lean)
1 shallot, minced
1 clove of garlic, minced
½ cup cooked rice
1 egg, beaten
½ tsp salt
½ tsp cumin
¼ tsp black pepper
2 tbsp fresh cilantro, chopped

1 medium red onion, diced
1 carrot, diced
2 stalks celery, sliced
1 tbsp canola oil
2 cloves garlic, minced
½ tsp salt
¼ tsp oregano
1 tsp chili powder
¼ tsp paprika
¼ tsp black pepper
32 oz chicken stock
3 large tomatoes, chopped
Fresh cilantro leaves for garnish

GLUTEN FREE

Cooking Instructions

Mix the beef, shallot, garlic, cooked rice, egg, salt, cumin, pepper and cilantro in a large bowl. Use a big table spoon to roll the meat mixture into balls and set them on a parchment paper-lined cookie sheet. You should have about 16-20 meatballs.

Start the soup by sautéing the onion, carrot and celery in the canola oil until fragrant, about 5 minutes. Add the garlic, salt, oregano, chili powder, paprika and pepper to the pot, and cook for 2 minutes, stirring constantly. Add the stock and the tomatoes to the pot, and bring to a simmer. Once a simmer is reached, turn the heat to low and drop the meatballs into the broth 4 or 5 at a time, then cook for 15 minutes until done. Then ladle the meatballs into individual bowls, 4 to 5 per bowl until all the meatballs are served. Taste the broth and adjust seasonings as needed with salt and pepper. Ladle the broth into the bowls and garnish with fresh cilantro.

Cook's Notes:

Like other meatball soups, be careful not to boil the meatballs or they will be tough. You're looking for a slow simmer for a gentle poach. Also pack the meatballs lightly rather than firmly to keep them tender.

Serves 4 | PREP TIME: 15 minutes. COOK TIME: 25 minutes.

NILA'S BEEF BORSCHT

This recipe was adapted from my mother-in-law, named Nila, from Ukraine. It's a hearty and warming soup she serves in the winter. I've made slight adjustments here and there, which she initially disapproved of. My version is slightly more savory and smoother. I also roast the beets, which takes longer but adds a nice dimension to the finished product. As she says "na zdorovye! [to your health]." Borscht is a big deal in her family, they take it seriously and my messing around with the recipe originally put me on thin ice, but now Nila says mine is better than hers, *spasiba* (thank you).

Ingredients

4 large beets, left whole and scrubbed well
(beet greens, sliced and reserved)
2 tbsp olive oil
Dash of salt

1 small yellow onion, diced
2 stalks of celery, sliced
2 carrots, sliced
1 tbsp butter
2 cloves garlic, minced
½ tsp salt
¼ tsp thyme
¼ tsp marjoram
¼ tsp black pepper
32 oz beef stock
1 lb bone-in beef shank
Salt and pepper to taste
Fresh dill fronds and sour cream for garnish

Cooking Instructions

Preheat oven to 350 degrees. Toss beets with 1 tablespoon of olive oil and a little salt in a large bowl. Turn out onto foil and wrap tightly. Place foil package in a pie pan and roast the beets for 1 to 1 ½ hours, or until tender. Check beets by piercing with the tip of a paring knife – finished beets will yield to the knife tip and be soft enough to slip out of their skins with a little pressure.

While the beets roast prepare the soup. Sauté the onion, celery and carrots in a large stockpot set over medium heat in the butter and the other tablespoon of olive oil until fragrant, about 8 minutes. Add the garlic, salt, thyme, marjoram and the pepper to the pot and cook for two minutes, stirring constantly. Add the stock and the beef shank and bring the soup to a simmer. Once a simmer is reached cover the pot and turn heat to low and continue cooking until the beef shank is tender, about 45 minutes to 1 hour. Remove the beef shank from the pot and set aside to cool. By now the beets should be done, so peel and quarter them before adding to the soup. Purée with an immersion blender or in your food processor in batches to a smooth consistency. Remove all bones and fat from the beef shank. Cut the meat into bite size pieces and add it and the sliced beet greens to the pot and cook for 25 minutes to allow all flavors to develop. Taste and adjust seasonings as necessary with salt and pepper as needed. Ladle into bowls and garnish with fresh dill and a dollop of sour cream.

GLUTEN FREE

Serves 4 – 6 | PREP TIME: 15 minutes. COOK TIME: 1 to 1½ hours.

ASIAN PORK & GLASS NOODLE SOUP

Bean-thread noodles are the prime component in this flavorful and easy soup with
a touch of lemongrass and the exotic flavor of Chinese five-spice powder.
It comes together quickly and makes for a sensational lunch.

Ingredients

1 medium onion, diced

1 carrot, diced

1 stalk celery, diced

1 tbsp canola oil

2 cloves garlic, minced

½ tsp salt

1 tbsp soy sauce

½ tsp Chinese five-spice powder

1 stalk of lemongrass, crushed and cut into
one-inch pieces

32 oz chicken stock

1 tbsp fish sauce

1 lb bean-thread noodles (or rice vermicelli)

1 lb pork loin, cut into thin matchsticks

Salt and pepper to taste

Fresh scallions thinly sliced for garnish

Cooking Instructions

Bring a large pot of salted water to a simmer over medium high heat. Keep hot while preparing the rest of the soup so it is ready to cook the noodles when you are.

Sauté the onion, carrot and celery in the canola oil in a large stockpot over medium heat until fragrant, about 5 minutes. Add the garlic, salt, soy sauce, Chinese five-spice powder and lemongrass to the pot and cook for 2 minutes, stirring constantly. Add the stock and fish sauce and bring to a simmer.

At this point you should drop the noodles into the hot water and finish the rest of the soup while the noodles are cooking. Follow the cooking time as indicated on the noodle packaging.

Once a simmer is reached in the soup pot, add the pork matchsticks to the hot broth and cook until just done, about 5-8 minutes. Ladle the bean-thread noodles into four bowls. Top with several ladles of the pork and broth, and garnish with fresh scallions.

Cook's Note:

I first had this as a cold salad and found it quite unusual and delicious. Adding my own touches along with more broth made this a tasty and easy soup to add to our repertoire.

Serves 4 | PREP TIME: 10 minutes. COOK TIME: 25 minutes.

TRADITIONAL VIETNAMESE PHO WITH BEEF & WITHOUT THE CRAZY STUFF

Pho has a special place in my life. My wife introduced me to Pho back in 2005 when we were courting. We had spent the previous night out drinking wine and even though we slept in, neither of us was feeling great. The next day, Kris turned to me and said "I have the best thing for hangovers. We're going to go get Pho!" She then informed me on the way over (while I was trying to not pay too much attention to her driving) that Pho is a spicy and flavorful beef noodle soup, and it's the national dish of Vietnam. I figured how bad could it be and walked into the place feeling like it might turn my day around. The menus weren't in English, and the place was packed with people speaking different languages. I thought to myself, "This place must be good."

My future wife ordered two big bowls of Pho for us, and we waited and sipped on sodas made with fresh lime. Our Pho arrived steaming hot and smelling like salvation. They serve Pho with little plates of bean sprouts, lime wedges, sliced jalapeno, fresh basil leaves and fresh culantro leaves (first time I'd had it and I loved it)—you add the garnishes you want. So I dumped in what I thought was an appropriate amount of each and then got my spoon. Kris was already digging in and raving about how good it was.

I thought so too. The broth was heavily scented with star anise, cinnamon and white pepper. It was very rich. The noodles were long, thin and swam just under the surface. Then I came across something that looked like road kill. Imagine my surprise when I looked up to see my future wife happily slurping what appeared to be the other half of the road kill across the table. "What is that you're eating?" I asked, trying to sound innocent and not freaked out.

"Oh this? Tendon! It's delicious."
"Hmmmm", I murmured, spooning bits of tendon out of my bowl. Then I uncovered what appeared to be a large square of the bleached interior of a basketball floating in my soup. As if on cue Kris was eagerly chawing on a piece of the very same material, holding it in her chopsticks all the while. "Tripe", she said. "Good for ya!"

I am highly sensitive to foreign textures and tastes when hung over, but that day I powered through every freaky, gelatinous, slimy, stringy, funky spoonful of Pho and it turned out that Kris was right, I did indeed feel a whole lot better. The spice from the peppers and the citrus lime with the deeply flavorful broth were not only delicious, but also brought me back to a state resembling normal. I've since discovered that Pho can be made with all manner of cuts of meat and that usually thin slices of beef sirloin are used in this recipe. The meat is cut very thin and then the boiling hot broth is poured over the meat and noodles once they are in the bowl, cooking the meat on its way to your table.

After that I became obsessed with trying to make the perfect pho. It's a time consuming process but all the steps are easy and the ingredients (save fresh culantro) are easy to find. Enjoy. It's still one of my favorites.

Ingredients

1 lbs beef-knuckle bones, with marrow

1 3-inch long cinnamon stick

4 star anise

2 tbsp brown sugar

4 whole cloves

1 lime, sliced

½ tsp salt

2 large onions, peeled and halved

1 3-inch piece of ginger, halved

2 tbsp fish sauce

2 tbsp soy sauce

2 tbsp chili paste

2 lbs beef sirloin tip, sliced thin (1/8 inch max, thinner if possible) against the grain

1 bunch of scallions, sliced

1 lb banh pho noodles (or rice vermicelli)

Fresh basil leaves, lime wedges, bean sprout, sliced jalapeno and culantro leaves for garnishes

Cooking Instructions

Put 2 quarts water in a large stockpot and set it on the stove, covered. Heat to a simmer and reserve this to cook the noodles when needed.

Place the beef bones in another large pot and cover with water. Add the cinnamon stick, star anise, brown sugar, cloves, lime and salt to the water. Bring to a boil and simmer for 1½ hours, skimming the fat that rises to the top. While that is cooking, char the onion and the ginger by holding the onion and the ginger over the open flame of your stove, using tongs. They don't have to be perfectly evenly charred on all sides, just slightly charred and semi-cooked. Add the charred onion and ginger to the beef bones in the pot and skim any fat or scum that rises to the surface. Charring adds an extra depth of flavor and is a step that should not be skipped.

Once the bones are cooked, strain the broth into another pot set over medium-high heat. Add the fish sauce, soy sauce and chili paste to the strained broth, and bring to a boil.

Cook the noodles in the heated water of the other stockpot according to package directions, and drain well.

Now its time to assemble the pho. Ladle the noodles into large deep bowls and top with several slices of raw sirloin, then cover with several ladles of the boiling hot broth. Garnish the bowls with fresh scallions and serve with other garnishes on small plates on the side. Feel better.

Cook's Note:

Taking any shortcuts with this recipe just isn't worth it.

Serves 8 | PREP TIME: 30 minutes. COOK TIME: 2 hours

SPICY BEEF WITH RAMEN NOODLE SOUP

For a while during school it seemed like I lived on Top Ramen. Looking back, it's easy to see why; it is tasty, cheap and ready in minutes, perfect for a busy college kid on the go. This version is entirely more wholesome but nearly as easy to make.

Ingredients

1 medium onion, diced
1 carrot, diced
1 stalk celery, diced
1 tbsp canola oil
1 clove of garlic, minced
½ tsp salt
1 tbsp soy sauce
1 tbsp chili paste
32 oz beef broth
1 tbsp fish sauce
1 lb ramen noodles (or rice vermicelli)
1 lb beef flank steak, cut across the grain into ⅛ inch slices
Fresh scallions, sliced for garnish

Cooking Instructions

Bring a large pot of salted water to a simmer over medium-high heat. Keep hot to cook noodles while preparing the rest of the soup.

Sauté the onion, carrot and celery in the canola oil in a large stockpot over medium heat until fragrant, about 5 minutes. Add the garlic, salt, soy sauce and chili paste, and cook for 2 minutes, stirring constantly. Add the beef broth and fish sauce, and bring to a simmer.

At this point drop the noodles into the hot water and cook the rest of the soup while the noodles are cooking.

Once a simmer is reached in the soup pot, add the flank steak to the hot broth, cooking until just done, about 5-8 minutes. Ladle the ramen noodles into four bowls. Top with several ladles of the beefy soup and garnish with fresh scallions.

Cook's Note:

This is a very basic but very enjoyable and comforting dish for me, a noodle soup version of a PB&J, if you will. I remember eating ramen in my first apartments with fondness though this version is more wholesome and tasty, and takes about the same time to cook.

Serves 4 | PREP TIME: 10 minutes. COOK TIME: 20 minutes

TIJUANA TACO SOUP

I have zero idea if Tijuana is famous for tacos. I don't mean to sound ignorant, but unlike other soup names, I chose the title because I like the alliteration of the Tijuana Taco title, not because I visited Mexico. This soup was created on a whim when I substituted leftover taco meat for regular ground beef while making chili. The results were so good I started improving the recipe to its current state, perfection, if I do say so myself. Garnish with a bit of sour cream, fresh scallions and shredded cheddar cheese, and Olé! or whatever they say in Tijuana.

Ingredients

1 lb ground beef (85% lean)
1 large red onion, chopped
2 carrots, sliced
2 stalks celery, sliced
1 tbsp canola oil
2 cloves garlic, minced
½ tsp salt
¼ tsp oregano
¼ tsp paprika
¼ tsp black pepper
32 oz chicken stock
1 tsp chili powder
10 oz cooked pinto beans
Salt and pepper to taste
Fresh scallions, sour cream and shredded cheddar cheese for garnishes

GLUTEN FREE

Cooking Instructions

Brown the ground beef in a skillet over medium heat until cooked through, about 10 minutes, stirring with a wooden spatula to break up the meat into crumbles. When finished drain and set aside.

In a large stockpot over medium heat, sauté the onion, carrots and celery in the canola oil until fragrant, about 5 minutes. Add the garlic, salt, oregano, paprika and pepper to the pot and cook for 2 minutes, stirring constantly. Add the stock, ground beef, chili powder and pinto beans and bring to a simmer. Once a simmer is reached reduce heat to low and continue cooking to develop the flavors for 15 minutes. Taste the soup and adjust seasonings as needed with salt and pepper. Ladle into bowls and garnish with fresh scallions, shredded cheddar and a dollop of sour cream.

Cook's Note:

I like to serve this with jalapeno cheddar corn bread. I have also garnished it with tortilla chips, and it was almost as good.

Serves 4 | PREP TIME: 10 minutes. COOK TIME: 25 minutes

SALVATORE'S SAUSAGE AND BARLEY SOUP

Sal was a wonderful, sweet man who lived next door to me in the Lakeview neighborhood of Chicago a decade ago. Always quick with a smile and good word, he was the kind of guy who'd look after your dog or make sure the mail didn't pile up when you were out of town. The neighborhood association organized a block party one fall and asked each of us to bring a dish. I was doing barbecue ribs; Sal brought this soup. I was blown away when I tried it. Nicely spiced sausage with carrot and onion, well balanced by the earthy quality of barley, and perfectly satisfying on a windy October day. Sal saw me greedily spooning up his soup and sauntered over with a smile. "You want the recipe, don't you?" he asked. "You're damned right I do!" I replied. "I want to put this on the menu at the Soupbox." And bless his heart he did provide the recipe. Sal said the secret was mild Italian sausage from Paulina Meat Market in Chicago. I agreed, and we've been using that same sausage to make this soup for the past ten years. This soup is well served with a light salad or half sandwich, and a big glass of Shiraz, though Sal prefers Chianti.

Ingredients

1 large onion, diced
1 large carrot, sliced
2 stalks celery, sliced
2 tbsp olive oil
3 cloves garlic, minced
2 tbsp tomato paste
1 tsp basil
½ tsp salt
½ tsp red pepper flakes
1 tsp oregano
1 tbsp parsley
½ tsp rosemary
1 lb mild Italian sausage (from Paulina Meat Market if you can get it)
8 oz red wine
40 oz beef stock
½ cup pearled barley
Salt and pepper to taste

Cooking Instructions

Sauté the onion, carrot and celery in the olive oil in a large stock pot set over medium heat until fragrant, about 8-10 minutes. Add the garlic, tomato paste, basil, salt, red pepper flakes, oregano, parsley and rosemary. Cook for one minute, stirring constantly. Add the Italian sausage and cook until browned, about 10 minutes. Drain the fat and return to medium heat. Add the wine and scrape the bottom of the pot with a spatula to get any browned bits off. Add the beef stock and bring to a simmer. Add the barley and cook, covered, for 25-30 minutes until the barley is tender. Stir often. Taste the soup and adjust seasonings as necessary with salt and pepper.

Serves 6-8 | PREP TIME: 10 minutes. COOK TIME: 50 minutes.

SOUTHERN COMFORT SOUP WITH SMOKED BACON & COLLARD GREENS

A long time ago I got into Southern cooking because I was looking for a go-to biscuit recipe to serve with a dynamite sausage gravy I make. Shortly after, the time-honored tradition of cooking and eating collard greens came into my life. Grits and fried chicken soon followed. Then came all things barbecue. After that I had a black-eyed pea dish at a friend's house on New Years Eve. It wasn't long until I put them all together in this soup; a hearty and soul-satisfying bowl of love that will have you whistling "Dixie" in no time!

Ingredients

8 oz smoked, thick-cut bacon, diced
1 large sweet onion, diced
2 medium carrots, sliced
1 stalk celery, sliced
1 tbsp canola oil
3 cloves garlic, minced
1 tsp thyme
1 tsp salt
1 tsp cayenne pepper
1 tsp oregano
2 tbsp tomato paste
1 head collard greens, washed, stems trimmed and chopped (about 6 cups)
1 tsp sugar
½ tsp sweet paprika
2 tbsp cider vinegar
48 oz chicken stock
16 oz black-eyed peas (soaked overnight)
Salt and pepper to taste

Note: You'll need to soak the peas overnight.

Cooking Instructions

Sauté the onion, carrot and celery with the bacon and canola oil in a large stockpot set over medium heat until the bacon is done and the onion are translucent, about 10 minutes. Add the garlic, thyme, salt, cayenne pepper, oregano and tomato paste. Cook for one minute, stirring constantly. Add the collard greens, sugar and paprika with the cider vinegar and 8 ounces of the stock. Stir well and cook uncovered for 10 minutes until the greens have started to wilt and the liquid has reduced to almost nothing. Add the remaining stock and black-eyed peas. Bring the soup to a simmer, cover and cook for 30-45 minutes until the black-eyed peas are tender. Taste the soup and adjust seasonings as necessary with salt and pepper.

GLUTEN FREE

Serves 6-8 | PREP TIME: 10 minutes. COOK TIME: 1 hour.

CHAPTER THREE

CHICKEN AND OTHER FEATHERED FRIENDS

Chicken soup is the quintessential soup dish. Most of us believe in its healing powers. In fact, science has shown that a good chicken soup has anti-inflammatory properties. But I bet the science effect is small compared to the mental one. Chicken soup makes people believe they are better which is half the task of feeling better.

Chicken soup is an ideal, an aspiration. It's also the core of our business. Its versatility attracts. It's quick and easy, and doesn't require a lot of prep. You don't need to brown the chicken which saves time. It's an easy and accommodating flavor and goes well with many different spices. Because of all this, we include a lot of chicken recipes in the book.

I recommend you don't mess with your chicken stock. At Soupbox we make a very basic one that is absolutely great and appealing to our customers. You know what you're getting. It's comforting. It's easy and friendly. It's chicken soup.

CREAMY CHICKEN AND WILD RICE SOUP

This is the number one selling soup at both our stores. It sells two-to-one over our best stuff.
It's the embodiment of your favorite chair or blanket, like a snuggy in a bowl.

Ingredients

1 medium onion, diced

1 medium carrot, diced

2 stalks celery, diced

½ cup butter

2 cloves garlic, minced

32 oz chicken stock

½ teaspoon thyme

½ teaspoon sage

1 cup uncooked wild rice

3 cups milk, more as needed

¼ cup all purpose flour

2 cups cooked, cubed chicken breast or thigh

Salt and pepper to taste

Cooking Instructions

In a large stockpot, sweat the onion, celery and carrot in the butter over medium heat until translucent, about 10 minutes. Add the garlic and cook two minutes longer. Add the chicken stock, thyme and sage along with the wild rice. Bring to a simmer and cook for 25 minutes with the lid on. Remove lid and check the doneness of the wild rice; if it's tender, proceed, if not, cover and cook for another ten minutes.

In the meantime whisk the milk and flour together. Once the wild rice is tender add the milk and flour mixture to the soup along with the cooked chicken. Bring up to a simmer for 15-20 minutes and allow the soup to thicken. Add salt and pepper to taste. Add more milk if the soup gets too thick.

Serves 6 | PREP TIME: 15 minutes. COOK TIME: 45 minutes.

HEALTHY ROSEMARY CHICKEN DUMPLING SOUP

This was an attempt to make a particularly healthy recipe. It is low in sodium and fat. We use a lot of herbs to boost the flavor, rosemary being a particularly strong one. However, it needed something to make it special so we added dumplings, and it became one of our most popular soups.

Ingredients

1 medium onion, diced
2 stalks celery, diced
1 medium carrot, diced
2 tbsp olive oil
2 cloves garlic, minced
32 oz chicken stock
2 cups cooked chicken, shredded
½ tsp thyme
1 tsp rosemary
2 bay leaves
Salt and pepper to taste

DUMPLINGS

1 ½ cups all-purpose flour
½ tsp salt
½ tsp baking powder
3 tbsp butter
1 egg, beaten
½ cup whole milk
Cold water as needed

Cooking Instructions

In a large stockpot, sweat the onion, celery, and carrot in the olive oil over medium heat for 10 minutes. Add the garlic and cook two minutes longer. Add the chicken stock, chicken and dried herbs. Bring the soup to a simmer and cook for 15 minutes with the lid on.

While the soup simmers, make the dumplings. Combine the flour, salt and baking powder in a mixing bowl. Mix in the butter and stir until well incorporated. Add egg and milk, and mix thoroughly. Mixture should be slightly wet; add cold water as needed to make the dough pliable. When the dough is finished drop spoonfuls into the warm (but not boiling) soup. The dumplings will cook in about ten minutes. Be careful to keep the soup under a boil or the dumplings will toughen. Add salt and pepper to taste and serve.

Serves 8 | PREP TIME: 25 minutes. COOK TIME: 40 minutes.

ROASTED CHICKEN FLORENTINE

The spinach and parmesan tortellini finished with a touch of whole milk make this a good, hearty soup and the perfect meal for a fall day.

Ingredients

1 medium onion, diced

2 stalks of celery, diced

1 carrot, diced

2 tbsp olive oil

1 tbsp flour

2 cloves of garlic, minced

½ tsp salt

¼ tsp thyme

¼ tsp black pepper

32 oz chicken stock

1 cup whole milk

2 cups fresh spinach, washed and trimmed

1 lb pre-roasted chicken, cubed

1 lb spinach and parmesan tortellini

fresh parsley for garnish

Cooking Instructions

Sauté the onion, celery and carrot in the olive oil in a large stockpot set over medium heat until translucent, about 8 minutes. Add the flour, garlic, salt, thyme and pepper, and cook for 2 minutes, stirring constantly. Add the stock and milk, and bring to a boil. Then add the spinach, cubed chicken and tortellini, and cook until done, about 10 minutes. Taste and adjust seasonings as necessary with salt and pepper. Garnish with fresh parsley and serve with toasted garlic bread.

Cook's Note:

You can make this with a stew-like texture by adding two tablespoons of flour instead of one.

Serves 4 | PREP TIME: 10 minutes. COOK TIME: 20 minutes.

ROASTED CHICKEN POT PIE SOUP

I make this soup when the first snow hits the ground. There's nothing better than delicious smells of homey cooking to drive out the chilly air. We serve it with freshly baked drop biscuits. I love to crumble them directly into the soup.

Ingredients

1 medium onion, diced

2 carrots, sliced

2 stalks celery, diced

2 tbsp butter

2 tbsp olive oil

2 cloves garlic, minced

½ tsp salt

½ tsp white pepper

½ tsp oregano

½ tsp thyme

2 bay leaves

1 tsp poultry seasoning

1 whole chicken, cut into 8 pieces

24 oz chicken stock

4 medium red skinned potatoes, cut into ½ inch chunks

1 cup green beans, cut into 1-inch pieces

1 tbsp corn starch mixed with 1 tbsp cold water

8 oz whole milk

1 cup English peas, fresh or frozen

Cooking Instructions

Melt the butter with the olive oil over medium heat in a large stockpot. Add the onion, carrot and celery, and cook until fragrant, about 5 minutes. Add the garlic, salt and all the dried spices, and cook for two minutes, stirring constantly. Add the chicken pieces and stock, and bring to a simmer. Then cover the pot and turn the heat to low. Cook covered for 45 minutes until the chicken is cooked through.

Remove the cooked chicken from the pot and set aside to cool. Add the potatoes and green beans, and cook until tender, about 20 minutes. When the chicken is cool enough, pull the meat from the bones and chop it into bite-sized pieces. Add the corn starch and cook for 5 minutes. Add the chopped chicken, milk and peas to the pot once the potatoes are tender, about 5 minutes. Taste the soup and adjust seasonings as needed with salt and pepper.

Serves 6-8 | PREP TIME: 20 minutes. COOK TIME: 1 hour 15 minutes.

CLASSIC CHICKEN NOODLE SOUP

When I was a young child, my grandmothers lived with us and took care of me in the afternoons. Then Bernadine got remarried, and Pearl had to go into an assisted-living home, and I was suddenly a latchkey kid. My dad was working at Caterpillar so was out very early and back late. I'd come home and be alone, so I'd make myself a can of chicken noodle soup. It was so comforting, I ate it nearly everyday. This is a simple re-creation of the classic favorite. I didn't want to mess with my memories.

Ingredients

1 medium onion, diced

2 medium carrots, diced

2 stalks celery, chopped

1 tbsp canola oil

2 cloves garlic, minced

1 sprig fresh thyme

2 bay leaves

1 tsp parsley

½ tsp marjoram

½ tsp salt

32 oz chicken stock

6 oz egg noodles

1 cup peas, fresh or frozen

2 cups cooked chicken, boneless, skinless thighs, cubed

Salt and pepper to taste

Cooking Instructions

Sauté the onion, carrots and celery in the canola oil over medium heat in a large stockpot until translucent, about 8-10 minutes. Add the garlic and dried herbs, and cook for 1 minute while stirring. Add the chicken stock and bring to a simmer. Then add the egg noodles and cook according to the package directions, about 7-10 minutes. Once the noodles are almost finished (al dente), add the peas and cooked chicken. Heat just long enough to warm them through, about 3 minutes. Taste and adjust seasonings with salt and pepper as needed.

(Do not use more - noodles expand + suck up broth)

Serves 6 | PREP TIME: 15 minutes. COOK TIME: 30 minutes.

TORTELLINI CON BRODO

Translated simply as 'tortellini in broth,' this wonderfully easy-to-make soup is very satisfying and comes together in minutes. Benissimo!

Ingredients

1 shallot, minced

1 stalk of celery, diced

1 carrot, diced

2 tsp olive oil

1 clove of garlic, minced

½ tsp salt

¼ tsp black pepper

48 oz chicken stock

1 lb of your favorite prepackaged tortellini (we use roasted chicken & ricotta)

Salt and pepper to taste

Fresh parsley, chopped for garnish

Cooking Instructions

Sauté the shallot, celery and carrot in the olive oil in a large stockpot set over medium heat until translucent, about 8 minutes. Add the garlic, salt and pepper to the pot and cook for two minutes, stirring constantly. Add the stock to the pot and bring to a boil. Once the soup reaches a boil, add the tortellini and cook per the package instructions. Taste and adjust seasonings as necessary with salt and pepper. Garnish with fresh parsley and serve.

Cook's Note:

I love this dish because it's so simple and easy yet still retains a homemade feel and flavor.

Serves 4 | PREP TIME: 10 minutes. COOK TIME: 20 minutes.

SICILIAN CHICKEN SOUP WITH BOWTIE PASTA

This is a soul satisfying chicken noodle soup kicked up with roasted red pepper and flat-leaf parsley. It makes a great lunch served with a salad and some fresh breadsticks.

Start w saute of chicken breasts — skin on brown on both side — Take out scrap up brown bits — then add onion etc

6 sprigs

Thyme

Ingredients

1 small yellow onion, diced
2 stalks of celery, diced (leaves included)
1 carrot, diced
2 tsp olive oil
2 cloves garlic, minced
½ tsp salt
¼ tsp basil
¼ tsp oregano
¼ tsp rosemary
¼ tsp black pepper
1 tbsp tomato paste
48 oz chicken stock
1 cup bowtie pasta
1 lb cooked chicken, cubed
2 tbsp flat-leaf Italian parsley, minced
Salt and pepper to taste
Fresh parsley, chopped for garnish

Cooking Instructions

Sauté the onion, celery and carrot in the olive oil in a large stockpot set over medium heat until translucent, about 8 minutes. Add the garlic, salt, basil, oregano, rosemary, pepper and tomato paste, and cook for two minutes, stirring constantly. Add the stock to the pot and bring to a boil. Then add the pasta and cook per the package instructions until al dente, about 8 minutes. When the pasta is done, stir in the chicken and parsley, and warm through, about 5 minutes longer. Taste and adjust seasonings as necessary with salt and pepper. Garnish with more fresh parsley.

Cook's Note:

This is one of the simplest and fastest recipes we have, and my daughter loves it. It's a nice spin on the classic chicken noodle soup.

Serves 4-6 | PREP TIME: 10 minutes. COOK TIME: 25 minutes.

SPICY MAYAN CHICKEN ENCHILADA

This is one of our newest soups, and I think it is a great one. The chipotle adds a little heat, and the queso fresco adds a smooth finish.

Ingredients

1 large onion, diced

2 carrots, diced

2 stalks celery, diced

1 tbsp canola oil

2 cloves garlic, minced

2 tsp ground cumin

2 tbsp chili powder

4 cups chopped fresh tomatoes or 2 (14.5 ounce) cans diced tomatoes

2 cups tomato sauce

1 chopped chipotle pepper

32 oz chicken stock

1 cup cooked black beans

1 cup corn kernels, fresh or frozen

2 cups cooked chicken, shredded

Salt and pepper to taste

4 oz crumbled queso fresco

Cooking Instructions

Warm the oil in a stockpot over medium heat. Add the onion, carrot and celery, and sauté until softened, about 10 minutes. Add the garlic and dry spices, and cook until fragrant, about one minute. Add the tomatoes, chipotle pepper and chicken stock. Bring to a simmer and cook for 15 minutes. Add the beans, corn and chicken. Return to a simmer and cook another 15 minutes to allow the flavors to develop. Taste and add salt or pepper as needed. Right before service, add the queso fresco and stir to combine.

Serves 8 | PREP TIME: 15 minutes. COOK TIME: 45 minutes.

CHICKEN AZTECA

The depth of flavor in this soup comes from dried pasilla and ancho chiles combined with a hint of lime. Almost stew-like; this recipe is equally at home as a lunch on a blustery day or as the main attraction at your Super Bowl party.

Ingredients

1 large red onion, diced
2 stalks of celery, diced
2 carrots, sliced
1 tbsp olive oil
3 cloves garlic, minced
½ tsp salt
½ tsp cumin
¼ tsp paprika
½ tsp oregano
¼ tsp epazote
¼ tsp chili powder
¼ tsp black pepper
4 dried pasilla peppers, rehydrated, seeded and chopped
4 dried ancho peppers, rehydrated, seeded and chopped
32 oz chicken stock
4 medium tomatoes, peeled, seeded and chopped
1 cup long grain white rice
1 lb roasted chicken, shredded
2 tbsp lime juice
Salt and pepper to taste
Fresh scallions and sour cream for garnish

Cooking Instructions

Sauté the onion, celery and carrots in a large stockpot set over medium heat in the olive oil until the onions are translucent, about 8 minutes. Add the garlic, salt, cumin, paprika, oregano, epazote, chili powder and pepper along with the pasilla and ancho peppers to the pot, and cook for two minutes, stirring constantly. Add the stock and tomatoes, and bring to a simmer. Once the soup reaches a simmer, add the rice, cover the pot and turn heat to low. Continue cooking until the rice is done, about 15-20 minutes. Then add the lime juice and shredded chicken, and warm through, about 3 minutes more. Taste and adjust seasonings as necessary with salt and pepper. Ladle soup into bowls and garnish with fresh scallions and a dollop of sour cream.

Cook's Note:

This is one of my all-time favorite soups. It's great through and through, with interesting and complex flavors. Works in a slow cooker, too.

Serves 4-6 | PREP TIME: 20 minutes. COOK TIME: 1 hour.

CHICKEN AND OTHER FEATHERED FRIENDS 109

AUTHENTIC MEXICAN TORTILLA SOUP

This was my first foray into ethnic soups. It has a nice medium body, a classic tomato and chicken-broth base and great Latin spices to give it some south-of-the-border pizazz.

Ingredients

1 large onion diced

1 stalk celery diced

1 carrot diced

2 tablespoons canola oil

2 cloves garlic, minced

4 cups fresh tomatoes, rough dice or 2 (14.5 ounce) cans diced tomatoes

32 oz chicken stock

1 chipotle pepper and 1 teaspoon of the adobo sauce they come packed in

1 teaspoon ground cumin

1 tablespoon ancho chile powder

1 cup cooked black beans

1 cup corn kernels, fresh or frozen

16 oz cooked chicken breast, ½ inch dice

Salt and pepper to taste

¼ cup chopped fresh cilantro

Juice from 2 limes

Cooking Instructions

Warm the canola oil in a stockpot over medium heat. Add the onion, carrot and celery, and sauté until just softened, about 5 minutes. Add the garlic, tomatoes, chicken stock and chipotle along with the cumin and chili powders. Bring the soup to a simmer and cook for 20 minutes. Add the beans, corn and chicken. Return to a simmer and cook for another 15 minutes to allow the flavors to develop. Taste and add salt or pepper as needed. Right before service, stir in the cilantro and lime juice.

Serves 6 | PREP TIME: 20 minutes. COOK TIME: 30 minutes.

OLD WEST CHICKEN ADOBO

Adobo is a old Spanish marinade that's become beloved throughout the world. Originally used as a way to preserve meats before the invention of refrigeration, adobo has resurfaced today because of its incredibly easy preparation and appealing flavor. It's important that the chicken be marinated for at least two hours, and preferably overnight. Then the rest of the dish comes together quickly.

Ingredients

MARINADE

Juice of 2 oranges

Juice of 1 lime

2 chipotle chiles from a can, chopped, plus about 1 tsp of the sauce they are packed in

4 cloves garlic, minced

1 tbsp cider vinegar

1 tbsp honey

1 tsp Hungarian paprika

1 tsp smoked Spanish paprika

½ tsp cumin

½ tsp salt

¼ tsp black pepper

2 lbs boneless, skinless chicken breast, cut into 1 inch chunks

SOUP

1 large red onion, diced

2 stalks of celery, diced (leaves included)

1 carrot, diced

2 tbsp canola oil

2 cloves garlic, minced

½ tsp salt

½ tsp cumin

1 tbsp tomato paste

SOUP INGREDIENTS (CONTINUED)

¼ tsp cayenne pepper

32 oz chicken stock

1 large potato, peeled and diced

1 large zucchini, sliced into half moons

1 cup sweet corn kernels, fresh or frozen

Fresh scallions and sour cream for garnish

Cooking Instructions

Whisk the marinade ingredients together in a large non-reactive bowl. Add the chicken and mix well. Cover and refrigerate for at least two hours and preferably overnight.

Once the chicken has marinated, sauté the onion, celery and carrot in the canola oil in a large stockpot set over medium heat until translucent, about 8 minutes. Add the marinated chicken and whatever marinade is left in the bowl to the pot, and cook until done, about 15 minutes, stirring occasionally. Add the garlic, salt, cumin, tomato paste and cayenne pepper, and cook for two minutes, stirring constantly. Add the stock to the pot and bring to a simmer. Then add the potatoes and zucchini, and cook for 15 minutes until the potatoes are tender. Stir in the corn and warm through, about 5 minutes longer. Taste and adjust seasonings as necessary with salt and pepper. Garnish each bowl with chopped fresh scallions and a dollop of sour cream.

Note: The cook and prep times do not include the marinating time, recommended to be overnight.

Serves 6 – 8 | PREP TIME: 10 minutes. COOK TIME: 35 minutes.

CANTONESE CHICKEN CHOWDER

Wonderfully flavorful and super quick to make, this departure from staid chicken soup recipes has proven very popular at our stores and with my daughter, Pearl (named after my grandmother). The many ingredients come together quickly and easily. The results are spectacular.

Ingredients

2 shallots, diced

2 stalks of celery, diced

2 carrots, sliced

1 tbsp olive oil

2 clove of garlic, minced

½ tsp salt

1 one inch piece of fresh ginger, peeled and sliced

½ tsp Chinese 5 spice powder

1 star anise

¼ tsp white pepper

48 oz chicken stock

8 oz thin rice noodles (mai sin)

1 lb cooked chicken, shredded

1 cup corn kernels, fresh or frozen

2 tbsp corn starch mixed with 2 tbsp cold water

Fresh scallions and lime wedges for garnish

Cooking Instructions

Sauté the shallots, celery and carrots in the olive oil in a large stockpot set over medium heat until translucent, about 8 minutes. Add the garlic, salt, ginger, 5-spice powder, star anise and white pepper to the pot and cook for two minutes, stirring constantly. Add the stock to the pot and bring to a boil. Once the soup reaches a boil add the mai sin (noodles) and cook until done, about 7 minutes. Add the chicken and corn kernels, and warm through, about 3 minutes more. Add the cornstarch and cook another 5 minutes. Taste and adjust seasonings as necessary with salt and pepper. Garnish with fresh scallions and serve with lime wedges on the side.

Serves 4-6 | PREP TIME: 10 minutes. COOK TIME: 30 minutes.

CARIBBEAN JERK CHICKEN CHOWDER

I love road trips and when I try something I like, I go home and attempt to replicate it. On one trip, I had jerk chicken in Tulsa, Oklahoma, of all places. I really liked it. I kept trying to make jerk chicken at home, couldn't quite get it right and ended up with a bunch of leftovers. So what did I do? I made a pretty darn good soup that I like to serve with corn muffins.

Ingredients

2 shallots, diced

2 stalks of celery, diced (leaves included)

2 carrots, sliced

1 tbsp olive oil

2 cloves garlic, minced

½ tsp salt

¼ tsp allspice

½ tsp thyme

¼ tsp pepper

32 oz chicken stock

Juice from 1 orange

Juice from 2 limes

1 tbsp cider vinegar

1 habanero pepper, seeds removed and diced

2 bone-in chicken breasts

2 bone-in chicken thighs

2 medium potatoes, peeled and cut into ½ inch chunks

1 tbsp honey, or to taste

2 ears of sweet corn, kernels cut from the cob

Salt and pepper to taste

Fresh parsley

Cooking Instructions

Sauté the shallots, celery and carrots in the olive oil in a large stockpot set over medium heat for 8 minutes. Add the garlic, salt, allspice, thyme and pepper, and cook for two minutes, stirring constantly. Add the stock, orange juice, lime juice, cider vinegar and habanero pepper, and bring to a simmer. Then add the chicken and cook for 30 minutes. Add the potatoes and cook until tender, about 15 minutes longer. Turn the heat to low, check to make sure the chicken is cooked through and remove to a plate. Add the honey to the chowder. Taste and adjust seasonings as necessary with salt and pepper or more honey. Take the meat off the bones and shred the chicken. Add the corn and shredded chicken to the chowder and warm through. Taste one final time to adjust seasonings if necessary. Garnish with fresh parsley.

Cook's Note:

This is a great departure from traditional creamy corn chowders. Whenever we have jerked chicken on our menu at home, my wife buys an extra chicken so we can make this chowder too.

Serves 4–6 | PREP TIME: 10 minutes. COOK TIME: 1 hour.

ROASTED TURKEY WITH EGG NOODLE SOUP

This soup is too good to make only once a year when you're trying to figure out what to do with leftover turkey! It's my father-in-law's favorite, and we make it at least once a month all-year round. We serve this with corn muffins and honey butter.

Ingredients

1 large Vidalia onion, diced
2 stalks of celery, diced
2 carrots, sliced
2 cloves garlic, minced
1 tbsp olive oil
½ tsp salt
¼ tsp thyme
¼ tsp marjoram
¼ tsp ground sage
¼ tsp black pepper
1 whole smoked turkey leg
48 oz chicken stock
1 16 oz package uncooked egg noodles
Salt and pepper to taste
Fresh parsley for garnish

Note: You may need to go to your local butcher to find or order a smoked turkey leg, especially off season.

Cooking Instructions

Sauté the onion, celery and carrots in the olive oil in a large stockpot set over medium heat until the onions are translucent, about 8 minutes. Add the garlic, salt, thyme, marjoram, sage and pepper, and cook for two minutes, stirring constantly. Add the turkey leg and stock, and bring to a simmer. Then cover the pot, turn the heat to low and continue cooking to allow the flavors to develop for 30 minutes. Remove the turkey leg with tongs and set aside to cool. Raise the heat and bring the soup to a boil. Add the egg noodles and cook per the package instructions, about 10 minutes. Shred the meat from the turkey leg while the noodles are cooking. Once the noodles are done, return the turkey meat to the pot and warm through, about 5 minutes more. Taste and adjust seasonings as necessary with salt and pepper. Ladle soup into bowls and garnish with fresh parsley.

Cook's Note:

This is another simple recipe proving that fifteen steps aren't necessary to get dinner on the table. The cooking time can be cut further if you shred the turkey-leg meat and don't cook it with the broth, which I've done before, but you'll sacrifice some flavor.

Serves 4-6 | PREP TIME: 10 minutes. COOK TIME: 45 minutes.

TURKEY & WILD MUSHROOM SOUP

This was one of our first turkey recipes and is still one of the best. It's the perfect way to turn leftover turkey into a destination meal for the family. Take your leftover roast turkey, add four different kinds of mushrooms and a touch of cream to create a hearty and wonderful soup that teases the taste buds. This is a great soup to serve in hot sourdough bread bowls.

Ingredients

1 small yellow onion, diced
2 stalks of celery, sliced
1 carrot, sliced
1 tbsp olive oil
2 cloves garlic, minced
½ tsp salt
¼ tsp thyme
¼ tsp ground sage
¼ tsp rosemary
¼ tsp black pepper
2 tbsp butter
4 oz fresh button mushrooms, sliced
4 oz fresh shitake mushrooms, sliced
4 oz fresh oyster mushrooms, sliced
4 oz fresh crimini mushrooms, sliced
32 oz chicken stock
1 large potato, peeled and diced
1 lb cooked turkey, cubed
Salt and pepper to taste
1 cup heavy cream
Fresh parsley, chopped for garnish

1/2 C half+half
1/2 C water

Cooking Instructions

Sauté the onion, celery and carrots in the olive oil in a large stockpot set over medium heat until fragrant, about 8 minutes. Add the garlic, salt, thyme, sage, rosemary and pepper, and cook for two minutes, stirring constantly. Add the butter and fresh mushrooms, and continue cooking until the mushrooms have given up their water, about 10-15 minutes longer. Add the stock and bring to a simmer. Then add the potatoes, cover the pot, turn heat to low and continue cooking until the potatoes are tender, about 15 minutes. Add the turkey and warm through, about 5 minutes more. Taste and adjust seasonings as necessary with salt and pepper. Remove from the heat and stir in the cream. Garnish with fresh parsley.

Cook's Note:

Sometimes at home I'll substitute leftover rice or small noodles for the potato; you're just looking for a bit of starch to lend the soup some body. Also the mushrooms can be any kind you'd like, Portobello, Maitake, Lion's Mane, or all one type. However, be sure to cook them long enough to get the liquid out so they give off the full potential of their wonderful, earthy flavor.

Add cayenne pepper when serving - nice topping

3/25/13 - Made ~ left over turkey carcass

Serves 4-6 | PREP TIME: 10 minutes. COOK TIME: 45 minutes.

TEX-MEX TURKEY & TOMATO SOUP

The wonderful and distinctive flavor of turkey is paired with tomatoes, avocado and smoky chipotle chiles, creating a soup light enough to serve with a salad for lunch yet hearty enough to serve with corn muffins for dinner.

Ingredients

1 large red onion, diced
2 stalks of celery, diced
1 carrot, sliced
1 tbsp olive oil
3 cloves garlic, minced
½ tsp salt
½ tsp cumin
¼ tsp paprika
¼ tsp black pepper
2 canned chipotle chiles, diced, plus 1 tsp of the adobo sauce they are packed in
32 oz chicken stock
3 large tomatoes, peeled, seeded and chopped
1 lb roasted turkey, shredded
1 cup corn kernels, fresh or frozen
Salt and pepper to taste
Fresh scallions, chopped and sliced avocado for garnish

Cooking Instructions

Sauté the onion, celery and carrot in the olive oil in a large stockpot set over medium heat until translucent, about 8 minutes. Add the garlic, salt, cumin, paprika, pepper and chipotles plus 1 tablespoon of the sauce they are packed in. Cook for 2 minutes, stirring constantly. Add the stock and tomatoes, and bring to a simmer. Once the soup reaches a simmer, add the shredded turkey and cook until the flavors develop, about 15 minutes. Add the corn kernels and warm through, about 3 minutes more. Taste and adjust seasonings as necessary with salt and pepper. Garnish with fresh scallions and sliced avocado.

Cook's Note:

This recipe came about as I was trying to think up new ways to offer turkey soups when turkey went through a particularly popular phase. I already had a chili with turkey but was still looking for a kind of chicken tortilla soup spinoff, and this beaut is what came out of it.

Serves 4-6 | PREP TIME: 10 minutes. Cook TIME: 25 minutes.

CLASSIC GREEK AVGOLEMONO

This wonderful broth-based soup is thickened with egg, has a great lemony zest to it and has been around for literally centuries for good reason.

Ingredients

1 shallot, minced
1 clove of garlic, minced
1 tbsp olive oil
48 oz chicken stock
½ tsp salt
¼ tsp white pepper
½ cup orzo or rice
2 eggs
Juice from 2 lemons
1 lb cooked boneless skinless chicken breast, shredded
Salt and pepper to taste
Fresh parsley and lemon wedge for garnish

Cooking Instructions

Sauté the shallot and garlic in the olive oil in a large stockpot set over medium heat for 2 minutes. Add the stock, salt and pepper, and bring to a boil. Once the soup is boiling, add the orzo and cook until done, about 7-10 minutes. Turn the heat to low. Crack the eggs into a large bowl and whisk until frothy, about 3-5 minutes. Add the lemon juice to the eggs and whisk until fully incorporated. Whisk a little of the hot broth, ½ cup at a time, into the egg and lemon-juice mixture until the mix is tempered, about 1.5 cups of broth total. Be sure to mix thoroughly after each time you add broth to keep the eggs from scrambling. Once the broth is whisked in and the eggs are tempered, add the egg mixture back to the pot and stir well. Do not allow the soup to reach a boil or the eggs will scramble. Add the shredded chicken and warm through. Taste the soup and adjust seasonings as necessary with salt and pepper. Garnish with fresh parsley and serve with wedges of lemon.

Cook's Note:

This soup is fairly simple and easy, but I scrambled the eggs the first few times I tried to make it. Done well this is one of my favorite soups with the acid of the lemon balanced by the salty richness from the broth. That said I have a lot of favorites. As you can see I get excited about great tasting soups.

Serves 4-6 | PREP TIME: 10 minutes. COOK TIME: 20 minutes.

ROASTED CHICKEN WITH PESTO & PINK LENTILS

This recipe is an adaptation of a dish I first had at Raw Bar, an excellent restaurant on Clark Street, not far north of Wrigley Field in Chicago. The interplay between the bright pesto, and the earthly roasted chicken and lentils is wonderful.

Ingredients

1 medium yellow onion, diced
2 medium carrots, diced
2 stalks celery, diced
1 tsp olive oil
2 cloves garlic, minced
½ tsp salt
¼ tsp freshly ground black pepper
40 oz chicken stock
8 oz boneless skinless chicken thighs, cubed
8 ox boneless skinless chicken breast, cubed
8 oz pink lentils, rinsed and picked over
4 tbsp pesto (see my recipe below)
Salt and pepper to taste
Parmesan shavings for garnish

GLUTEN FREE

Cooking Instructions

Sauté the onion, carrot and celery in the oil in a large stock pot set over medium heat until fragrant, about 5 minutes. Add the garlic, salt and pepper, and cook for 1 minute, stirring constantly. Add the stock, and bring to a simmer. Then add the chicken and lentils. Cook uncovered for 30-40 minutes until the chicken is done and the lentils are tender. Remove from the heat and stir in the pesto. Taste the soup and adjust seasonings as necessary with salt and pepper. Garnish with parmesan shavings and serve.

Cook's Note:

Here's my recipe for Easy Peasy Pesto:

2 cups fresh basil (packed)
3 cloves garlic
½ cup grated parmesan cheese
⅓ cup pine nuts (or walnuts or almonds)
½ tsp salt
¼ tsp freshly ground black pepper
½ olive oil

Put all the ingredients save the olive oil in a food processor and pulse till combined. Slowly drizzle olive oil through the top with the processor on; pesto will thicken as theoil is added. Makes about 1 cup. Refrigerate leftovers.

Serves 4-6 | PREP TIME: 10 minutes. COOK TIME: 45 minutes.

TASMANIAN DUCK SOUP

Many years ago I was lucky enough to spend some time in Tasmania, which is a little island off the southern coast of Australia. Tasmania is a beautiful island that produces high-quality meat, seafood, and niche market items like honey and truffles. This recipe is an adaptation of a soup I enjoyed during my stay. The interplay between the savory duck and sweet apple gives this dish its interesting and appealing flavor.

Ingredients

2 shallots, diced
2 stalks celery, diced
1 carrot, sliced
1 tbsp olive oil
2 cloves garlic, minced
½ tsp salt
½ tsp thyme
¼ tsp black pepper
2 tbsp tomato paste
2 tomatoes, peeled, seeded and chopped
32 oz chicken stock
1 large apple, peeled and diced
1 large potato, peeled and diced
Pinch saffron threads
1 lb cooked duck meat, cubed
Salt and pepper to taste
Fresh parsley, chopped for garnish

Cooking Instructions

Sauté the shallots, celery and carrots in the olive oil in a large stockpot set over medium heat until fragrant, about 5 minutes. Add the garlic, salt, thyme, pepper, tomato paste and tomatoes, and cook for 2 minutes more, stirring constantly. Add the stock and bring to a simmer. Then add the apples, potatoes, saffron and duck, and cook until the potatoes are tender, about 15 minutes. Taste the soup and adjust seasonings as necessary with salt and pepper. Garnish with fresh parsley and serve.

Serves 4 | PREP TIME: 15 minutes. COOK TIME: 30 minutes.

TURKEY SOUP WITH CHORIZO, POTATOES AND LEEKS

This soup is a snapshot in time nearly a half decade ago. We had invited a lot of guests for Thanksgiving and spent all our money making the house and meal just right. We had a good turnout from both our families plus six store employees. Food and drink were plenty, and everyone left happy and sated with a nice plate of leftovers. However, I wasn't scheduled to get paid for another few days, and we'd just paid all our bills. This meant it was us versus the leftovers until the next check arrived. I used all my creative thinking powers. We had turkey and mushroom stir-fry, turkey and broccoli crown pizza (made with cheddar and gouda from the cheese plate) and turkey tetrazzini casserole. We were still counting the days until payday. Of course soup made the most sense. I surveyed the fridge and pantry to see what we had left; chorizo from the cheese plate, two cans of tomatoes, a lone leek rattling in the crisper drawer, a couple potatoes, and of course, turkey. I settle in and sharpened a knife; it was soup for dinner tonight!

Ingredients

1 large leek, washed and cut into ¼" slices

8 oz Spanish chorizo, cut into ¼" coins

2 tbsp olive oil

2 cloves garlic, minced

½ tsp thyme

1 tsp salt

½ tsp white pepper

1 tsp oregano

1 tbsp parsley

8 oz white wine

32 oz chicken stock

2 cans diced tomatoes (or 2 medium tomatoes, chopped)

1 lb cooked turkey

2 medium potatoes, cut into chunks

Salt and pepper to taste

Cooking Instructions

Sauté the leek and chorizo in the olive oil in a large stockpot set over medium heat until fragrant, about 5 minutes. Add the garlic, thyme, salt, pepper, oregano and parsley. Cook for one minute, stirring constantly. Add the wine and scrape the bottom of the pot with a spatula to get any browned bits off. Add the stock and tomatoes. Bring to a simmer and add the turkey and potatoes. Cover and cook for 20 minutes until the potatoes are tender. Taste the soup and adjust seasonings as necessary with salt and pepper.

This soup, along with some naan we had in the freezer and a bottle of Lambrusco left over from Thanksgiving dinner fed us well for the next two days. Once paid, we stuck a $20 bill in the dust cover of our favorite cookbook so we'd never be stuck staring down a week's worth of leftover turkey again! Funnily enough, we still eat the soup with some regularity even when there is money in the bank.

Serves 8 | PREP TIME: 10 minutes. COOK TIME: 30 minutes.

BETTY ANN'S FAMOUS DUCK SOUP

Betty Ann is my business partner, Jamie's mother. She has helped a lot over the years, providing support and different perspectives on life and business. She also contributed this terrific recipe. Hearty and full of flavor, this is the kind of soup you would make for a visiting dignitary or head of state. Serve with freshly baked multigrain rolls and a glass of Pinot Noir or Shiraz.

Ingredients

1 medium sweet onion, diced
1 large carrot, sliced
1 stalk celery, sliced
1 tbsp butter
1 tbsp olive oil
2 cloves garlic, minced
1 tsp thyme
1 tsp salt
½ tsp black pepper
1 tsp marjoram
2 tbsp tomato paste
40 oz chicken stock
½ cup pearled barley
4 oz mushrooms, sliced
1 bunch kale, stemmed and cut into ribbons
1 lb cooked duck meat, shredded
Salt and pepper to taste

Cooking Instructions

Sauté the onion, carrot and celery in the butter and olive oil in a large stockpot set over medium heat until fragrant, about 5 minutes. Add the garlic, thyme, salt, pepper, marjoram and tomato paste. Cook for one minute, stirring constantly. Add the stock and bring to a simmer. Add the barley, mushrooms and kale. Cover and cook for 25-30 minutes until the barley is tender. Add the duck and heat through, about 5 minutes more. Taste the soup and adjust seasonings as necessary with salt and pepper.

Serves 8 | PREP TIME: 10 minutes. COOK TIME: 45 minutes.

CHAPTER FOUR

CREAMY, CHEESEY OR TOMATO-Y SOUPS AND BISQUES

These soups are comfort in a spoon. When someone comes into the shop and has a cold, I give them samples of the chicken soup and vegetable soups. However, invariably they go for the cream of broccoli because it's comforting, and being comfortable helps a person heal.

Bisque is one of my favorite soups. It has a smooth and nice mouth feel. Also, it is a fancy reclamation project. A bisque uses heat to transform small pieces of traditionally leftover food into something amazing that captures the essence of the flavor in a distinctive, elegant and smooth meal.

A couple of practical notes for this chapter: When a soup recipe calls for cheese, be careful not to add it all at once. Stir it well while it's being added so it doesn't become stringy in the soup. Also make sure you add the cheese, or cream for that matter, off the heat. If either is subjected to too high a temperature, it will break which means the the fat will separate, and you will get oily spots on the top and the rest at the bottom.

These soups are some of our most popular at Soupbox. They're the richest, and fill you up while warming your bones.

SIGNATURE LOBSTER BISQUE

This dish is very rich and decadent. It doesn't use large chunks of lobster; just the essence of lobster in the tradition of a true bisque, and it's one of our most popular soups.

Ingredients

1 medium onion, diced

1 medium carrot, diced

2 stalks celery, diced

1 clove of garlic, minced

4 tbsp butter, divided

2 bay leaves

½ tsp dried thyme

1 cup white wine

1 whole 2 lb lobster, cooked and shelled, claw and tail meat removed and cut into small dice (reserve the rest of the lobster including the shell)

32 oz chicken stock

2 tbsp flour

2 tbsp tomato paste

1 cup heavy cream

¼ cup sherry

Salt and pepper to taste

Cooking Instructions

In a large pan, sauté the onion, carrot, celery and garlic in 2 tablespoons of butter over medium-high heat. Sweat the aromatics until translucent, about 6-8 minutes. Add the bay leaves and thyme, and stir for 1 minute. Deglaze the pan with the wine, then add the reserved lobster and shells, and cook for another 5 minutes. Add half the chicken stock and bring to a boil. Allow the soup to reduce for 5 minutes. Turn off the heat and transfer the entire batch to a stockpot; pouring the soup through a fine-mesh strainer, and pushing down with a spatula to insure you extract every last bit of flavorful stock. Melt the rest of the butter in a small saucepan on medium heat and add the flour, stirring constantly for 5 minutes until brown and incorporated. (You're making a roux to thicken the bisque.) While the roux is cooking add the tomato paste and the rest of the chicken stock to the bisque in the stockpot over medium heat. Add the finished roux to the bisque all at once and stir thoroughly. Allow the soup to come to a simmer. The soup will thicken as it cooks. Then remove it from the heat and add the cream, sherry and reserved lobster meat. Taste and adjust seasonings as needed with salt and pepper.

Serves 8 | PREP TIME. 15 minutes. COOK TIME. 35 minutes.

BROCCOLI & WHITE CHEDDAR SOUP

Our customer base is about 60 percent female. Of the 60 percent at least 70 percent will order our broccoli cheese soup. I think it's because women love cheese, and the broccoli makes it sound healthy. Anyway, I can see the appeal, but I'm biased.

Ingredients

1 medium onion, diced

1 medium carrot, diced

2 heads broccoli, cut into florets with stems peeled and cut into a small dice

4 tbsp butter

2 cloves garlic, minced

½ tsp thyme

¼ tsp marjoram

½ tsp salt

4 tbsp all-purpose flour

32 oz vegetable stock

16 oz whole milk

3 cups grated white cheddar cheese

Salt and pepper to taste

Cooking Instructions

In a large stockpot with a lid, sweat the onion, carrot and diced broccoli stems in 2 tablespoons of the butter over medium heat until translucent, about 10 minutes. Add the garlic and cook 2 minutes longer. Add the dried herbs, the rest of the butter and all of the flour, and stir well. Cook for 3-5 minutes until the flour is well incorporated, stirring constantly. Add the chicken stock and milk, and bring to a simmer. Add the broccoli florets and allow the soup to cook at a simmer for 20 minutes; it will thicken as it cooks. Then remove the soup from the heat and add the cheese, one cup at a time, stirring constantly to make sure it melts smoothly. Then taste the soup and adjust with salt and pepper as needed. Thin with a little more milk if desired.

Cook's Note:

You need to stir this soup like a madman when you first add the flour and when the cheese hits the flour later. Otherwise it will burn, and you will have to start the process over.

Serves 8 | PREP TIME: 20 minutes. COOK TIME: 40-45 minutes.

CHICKPEA CHOWDER WITH PURSLANE & LEEKS

Purslane is a wild green that become popular in the food industry a few years ago. I left it on the recipe list because it has a sharp, bitter green flavor like a peppery augula that gives the soup a good zippy flavor.

Ingredients

2 leeks, root and tops removed, sliced
1 medium carrot, diced
2 stalks celery, diced
2 tbsp olive oil
2 cloves garlic, minced
1 tsp thyme
2 bay leaves
32 oz vegetable stock
1 tsp salt
1 pinch red pepper flakes
2 cups chickpeas, soaked overnight
1 large potato, medium dice
1 bunch purslane, chopped *
Salt and pepper to taste

Note: You'll need to soak the chickpeas overnight.

Cooking Instructions

Sauté the leeks, carrot, and celery in the oil in a stockpot over medium heat until translucent; about 10 minutes. Add the garlic and dried herbs, and cook for one minute. Add the vegetable stock, salt and red pepper flakes, and bring to a simmer, stirring occasionally. When the soup has reached a simmer, add the chickpeas and potato, and cook until tender, approximately 25-30 minutes. Once the potato and the chickpeas are tender, add the purslane and cook for 5 minutes longer. Taste the soup and adjust seasonings with salt and pepper as needed.

Cook's Note:

You can substitute one bunch of spinach or kale for the purslane if it's not available.

Serves 6 | PREP TIME: 10 minutes. COOK TIME: 45 minutes.

BEER & CHEESE WITH SMOKED BACON SOUP

I was visiting Milwaukee Wisconsin years and years ago and went to a gimmicky bar called the Safe House, which is still there and still hidden behind a secret entrance. To me everything was overpriced and hokey, but they had this beer and cheese soup that was great and inspired me. It's a really popular soup at our stores, and the staff likes to mix it with our chili for yet another excellent flavor sensation.

Ingredients

1 medium onion, diced
2 stalks celery, diced
1 medium carrot, diced
2 tbsp olive oil
2 cloves garlic, minced
12 oz beer, any medium-body brew will work
24 oz chicken stock
8 oz cooked smoked bacon, chopped

4 tbsp butter
4 tbsp all-purpose flour
24 oz whole milk
5 cups grated cheddar cheese
1 tbsp spicy mustard
2 tsp hot sauce
Salt and pepper to taste

Cooking Instructions

In a large stockpot with a lid, sweat the onion, celery, and carrot in the butter over medium heat until translucent, about 10 minutes. Add the garlic and cook two minutes longer. Add the beer and stir well, then add the chicken stock and bacon. Bring to a simmer and cook for 15 minutes and remove from heat.

While the vegetables and beer are cooking, make the cheese base in another large pot with a heavy bottom. Melt the butter over medium heat and add the flour all at once. Stir constantly as the flour cooks and starts to darken slightly. Stir in the milk a cup at a time and keep the mixture moving to avoid scorching the roux, for about a minute or two. The mixture will thicken as it heats. Once the last cup of milk is incorporated remove the mixture from the heat and stir in the grated cheese one cup at a time until incorporated.

Over low heat, mix the vegetables and beer into the cheese base one cup at a time, making sure to stir thoroughly after each addition. Add mustard and hot sauce. Taste and adjust seasoning with salt and pepper as desired.

Serves 8 | PREP TIME: 20 minutes, COOK TIME: 40 minutes.

THE DIVINE CREAM OF MUSHROOM SOUP

This is a decadent soup for lunch as well as a wonderful treat as a first course in a special meal.
I think it is one of our best.

Ingredients

16 oz button mushrooms, sliced
1 tsp salt
2 tbsp olive oil
4 medium shallots, thinly sliced
3 cloves garlic, minced
2 tbsp butter
5 tbsp flour
6 cups chicken stock
2 tsp thyme
2 tsp parsley
½ cup heavy cream
Salt and pepper to taste

Cooking Instructions

Heat the olive oil in a large pot over medium-high heat. Add the mushrooms and a tsp of salt, and cook, stirring occasionally until soft, about 6 minutes. Add the shallots and cook, stirring occasionally, another 3 minutes. Add the garlic and cook for another 3 minutes. Stir in the butter. Add the flour and cook, stirring constantly, for 2 minutes more. Pour in the broth, and bring to a boil while stirring. Add the thyme and parsley, and lower the heat to medium low. Simmer for 10 minutes. Whisk the heavy cream into the soup and season with salt and pepper to taste.

Cook's Note:

People don't eat mushrooms often enough and then don't cook them long enough. You want to cook them to get the water out so the concentrated flavors can mingle nicely with the other spices and sauces in the dish. Don't skimp on the six-minute sauté time, it's worth it.

Serves 6 | PREP TIME: 15 minutes. COOK TIME: 25 Minutes.

CHIPOTLE SWEET-POTATO BISQUE

Warm and comforting, this easy bisque gets a flavor charge from spicy and savory canned chipotle chiles. The chipotles lend a smoky and spicy counterpoint to the earthy sweet potatoes. I like this garnished with a bit of sour cream and fresh parsley.

Ingredients

2 large carrots, diced
3 shallots, diced
2 stalks celery, diced
2 tbsp olive oil
2 cloves garlic, minced
1 canned chipotle, chopped, plus 1 tsp of the adobo sauce they are packed in
½ tsp oregano
½ tsp salt
¼ tsp freshly ground black pepper
32 oz vegetable stock
2 large sweet potatoes, peeled and quartered
2 Yukon Gold potatoes, peeled and quartered
Salt and pepper to taste

Cooking Instructions

Sauté the carrot, shallot and celery in a large stockpot set over medium heat until fragrant, about 5 minutes. Add the garlic, chipotle, oregano, salt and pepper, and cook for one minute, stirring constantly. Add the stock and bring the soup to a simmer. Then add the potatoes and cook until the potatoes are tender, about 30 minutes. Pulse with an immersion blender or blend in batches in your food processor until smooth. Taste the soup and adjust seasonings as necessary with salt and pepper.

Cook's Note:

If you'd like it a bit spicier, add another chipotle.

VEGAN FAVORITE

GLUTEN FREE

Serves 4-6 | PREP TIME: 10 minutes, COOK TIME: 45 minutes.

CREAM OF POTATO AND LEEK SOUP

This is a classic flavor combination inspired by the cold French soup vichyssoise and one of our oldest recipes. When we were testing this, I was trying to get the flavor of a sour cream and onion potato chip, which I love. I think we got there. I eat this soup the most often, maybe next to chili (and sometimes I mix the chili with the soup).

Ingredients

1 leek, chopped, including the green part

1 stalk celery, chopped

1 carrot, shredded

2 cloves garlic, minced

4 tbsp of butter

¼ cup all-purpose flour

2 cups chicken stock

3 potatoes cut in ¼ inch cubes

2 cups milk

1 tablespoon chopped fresh parsley

¼ teaspoon thyme

¼ teaspoon rosemary

Dash of hot sauce (like Tabasco sauce)

Dash of Worcestershire sauce

Salt and pepper to taste

Cooking Instructions

In a large stockpot, sweat the leek, celery, carrot, and garlic in the butter over medium heat, until just softened. Add the flour and stir constantly for 2 or 3 minutes. Add the chicken stock into the pot slowly, stirring as you add. Add the potatoes, milk, parsley, thyme, rosemary, hot sauce, and Worcestershire. Simmer for 20 to 30 minutes, stirring frequently, until the potatoes are soft.

Serves 6 | PREP TIME: 20 minutes. COOK TIME: 35 minutes.

ROASTED CORN & GREEN-CHILI CHOWDER

This easy and versatile chowder represents the coming fall for me each year; the last of the sweet corn and sun-kissed peppers rounded out by potato and cumin, with a touch of sweet cream. Garnished with fresh cilantro and served with crunchy corn muffins, this makes a great way to appreciate the last of the summer's blessings.

Ingredients

4 ears sweet corn
1 medium onion, diced
2 stalks celery, diced
1 carrot, sliced
2 tbsp olive oil
½ tsp salt
4 cloves garlic, minced
1 bay leaf
½ tsp cumin
½ tsp oregano
¼ tsp allspice
¼ tsp white pepper
4 large poblano peppers, roasted, peeled and seeded (or 3 cans roasted chiles)
2 medium potatoes, peeled and cut into ½ inch chunks
24 oz vegetable stock
Salt and pepper to taste
1 cup heavy cream
Fresh cilantro, chopped, and sour cream for garnish

Cooking Instructions

Preheat oven to 400 degrees. Leave the corn in the husks but pull off any dry tassels so they don't catch fire. Set the corn on the top rack of oven and roast for 30 minutes.

Prep the rest of the chowder while the corn is roasting. Sauté the onion, celery and carrot in the olive oil in a large stockpot set over medium heat until fragrant, about 5 minutes. Add the salt, garlic and dried spices, and cook for two minutes, stirring constantly. Add the chopped chiles, potatoes and vegetable stock, and bring to a simmer. Simmer uncovered until the potatoes are tender, about 20-25 minutes.

Remove the corn from the oven and let it cool slightly. Husk the corn (careful, it will be hot), cut it from the cobs and set aside.

Purée the soup with an immersion blender or in batches in your food processor. This step is not essential but helps make the final dish more smooth and creamy.

Add the corn, taste the soup and adjust seasonings as necessary with salt and pepper. Remove from heat and stir in the cream. Ladle into bowls and garnish with fresh chopped cilantro and a dollop of sour cream, and serve.

GLUTEN FREE

Serves 4 – 6 | PREP TIME: 20 minutes COOK TIME: 45 minutes

ROASTED GARLIC SCAPE BISQUE

When garlic plants send up their first flower shoots, farmers may cut them off to increase the size of the garlic heads harvested in the fall. Until recently, most of these treasures have been thrown away or relegated to the compost heap. However, now garlic scapes are widely available at farmer's markets for a few short weeks each spring. They make wonderful additions to stir fries or salads but are also dynamite in pestos and soups such as this one.

Ingredients

1 lb garlic scapes, cut into 1-inch pieces
2 tbsp olive oil, divided
2 medium carrots, quartered
1 small onion, diced
1 stalk celery, diced
1 large potato, peeled and diced
2 bay leaves
¼ tsp thyme
½ tsp salt
32 oz chicken stock
Salt and pepper to taste
1 cup heavy cream

Cooking Instructions

Heat oven to 400 degrees. Toss the scapes and the carrots in 1 tablespoon of the olive oil and turn out onto a foil-lined baking sheet. Roast the scapes and the carrots in the oven until just softened and starting to color, about 15 minutes. While the scapes are roasting, sauté the onion, celery and potato in the other tablespoon of olive oil in a large stockpot over medium heat until the onions are translucent, about 10 minutes. Add the dried herbs, salt and chicken stock, and bring to a simmer. Remove the scapes and carrots from the oven and add to the stockpot. Simmer all ingredients until they are soft, about 15 minutes longer. Remove the soup from the heat and purée with an immersion blender or in your food processor in batches until smooth. Taste the soup and adjust seasonings with salt and pepper then stir in the heavy cream.

Serves 6 | PREP TIME: 10 COOK TIME: 35 minutes.

ROASTED TOMATO & RED PEPPER BISQUE

Roasting vegetables is a quick and simple way to bring out their inherent natural sweetness as in the simple recipe. At home, we like to garnish this with a dollop of sour cream or plain yogurt to set off the color and add a bit of creaminess.

Ingredients

2 lbs fresh Roma or other plum tomatoes, cut in half and seeded

3 large red peppers, cut in half and seeded

1 medium onion, quartered

1 medium carrot, quartered

½ tsp salt

2 tbsp olive oil

2 bay leaves

¼ tsp thyme

¼ tsp oregano

¼ tsp basil

32 oz chicken stock

Salt and pepper to taste

GLUTEN FREE

Cooking Instructions

Heat oven to 425 degrees. Toss the tomatoes, peppers, onions and carrots in the salt and olive oil them turn out onto a foil-lined baking sheet. Roast the vegetables in the oven until softened, about 25 minutes. Remove the roasted vegetables, place in a large bowl and cover tightly for 10 minutes. Once the vegetables have cooled enough to touch, remove the skins from the peppers and put everything into a large stockpot set over medium heat. Add the dried herbs and chicken stock, and bring to a simmer. Then cook for an additional 15 minutes, stirring occasionally. Remove the soup from the heat, take the bay leaves out, and purée with an immersion blender or your food processor in batches to a smooth consistency. Taste the soup and adjust seasonings with salt and pepper as needed.

Cook's Note:

You may need to pass this soup through a strainer to get all the bits of tomato and pepper skins out for an extra smooth consistency as we do at Soupbox, though I don't do this all the time at home.

Serves 6 | PREP TIME. 10 COOK TIME. 50 minutes.

RUSTIC CAULIFLOWER & CABBAGE CHOWDER

A hearty and warming way to use up the autumn harvest, this chowder is surprisingly light while filling. The color contrast between the cauliflower, tomatoes and the cabbage also makes this an attractive dish. I like to serve it with shavings of Spanish Mahon cheese and breadsticks fresh out of the oven.

Ingredients

1 medium onion, diced

2 stalks celery, diced

2 carrots, diced

2 tbsp canola oil

½ tsp salt

2 cloves garlic, minced

2 bay leaves

1 tsp paprika

¼ tsp thyme

¼ tsp red pepper flakes

Pinch of caraway seeds

4 large fresh tomatoes, peeled, seeded and chopped

2 tbsp tomato paste

32 oz vegetable stock

2 large potatoes, cut into ½ inch chunks

1 head cauliflower, cut into 1-inch chunks

1 head green cabbage, cut into 1-inch chunks

1 cup English peas, fresh or frozen

Cooking Instructions

Sauté the onion, celery and carrot in the canola oil in a large stockpot set over medium heat until fragrant, about 5 minutes. Add the salt, garlic and dried spices to the pot, and cook for two minutes, stirring constantly. Add the tomatoes, tomato paste and stock, and bring the soup to a simmer. Then add the potatoes, cauliflower and cabbage, and turn the heat to low. Cover and continue cooking until everything is tender, about 20-30 minutes. Add the peas and warm through. Taste the soup and adjust seasonings with salt and pepper.

VEGAN FAVORITE

GLUTEN FREE

Serves 4-6 | PREP TIME: 20 minutes. COOK TIME: 40 minutes.

AVOCADO & ARTICHOKE BISQUE

We grew artichokes last year for the first time, due in large part to my wife's lust for them grilled and dipped in a lemon-pepper butter I make. The planting was done by my wife and three-year-old daughter, who was sowing seeds for the first time. A veritable forest of artichokes sprouted, and they were coming out of our ears as a result. I made this bisque on a lark with ingredients we had on hand and loved the results. I think you will, too.

Ingredients

1 medium leek, washed and sliced into ¼ inch half moons

2 carrots, sliced

2 stalks celery, sliced

2 tbsp butter

2 cloves garlic, minced

½ tsp thyme

2 bay leaves

6 medium artichokes, blanched and chokes removed, cut into 1-inch chunks (or two 14.5oz cans of artichokes)

2 large avocados, halved and interior flesh cut into cubes

32 ounces vegetable stock

Juice of one lemon

1 tsp lemon zest

Salt and pepper to taste

1 1/2 cups crème fraiche for garnish

Croutons for garnish

Cooking Instructions

Sauté the leeks, carrots and celery in the butter over medium-low heat in large stockpot until the onions are translucent, about 8-10 minutes. Add the garlic and herbs. Cook for 1 minute, stirring constantly. Add the artichokes and vegetable stock. Bring to a simmer, cover and turn heat to low. Cook for 10 minutes until the flavors have developed. Add the avocados, lemon juice and lemon zest. Remove from the heat. Taste and adjust seasonings with salt and pepper as needed. Take out the bay leaves and puree with an immersion blender to a smooth consistency. You may need to pass this soup through a strainer to get all the bits of artichoke fiber out for a smooth consistency, though that won't be necessary if you are using canned artichokes. Garnish each bowl with ¼ cup crème fraiche and top with croutons and serve.

Serves 6 | PREP TIME: 10 minutes. COOK TIME: 25 minutes.

SUNCHOKE BISQUE WITH ROASTED SWEET PEPPERS

Sunchokes (also called Jerusalem artichokes) are the tuber-like root of sunflowers. I first came across them at a farmers market a couple of years ago. They have a slightly nutty and sweet flavor and make a great base for this bisque. The sweetness of the peppers contrasts nicely with the earthy sunchokes.

Ingredients

2 shallots, sliced

2 tbsp butter

2 cloves garlic, minced

1 tsp parsley

½ tsp marjoram

24 ounces vegetable stock

1 lb sunchokes, washed and quartered

2 yukon potatoes, washed and quartered

1 cup heavy cream

Salt and pepper to taste

1 cup roasted sweet red peppers

Cooking Instructions

Sauté the shallots in the butter over medium-low heat in a large stockpot until translucent, about 8-10 minutes. Add the garlic and herbs. Cook for 1 minute, stirring constantly. Add the vegetable stock and bring to a simmer. Add the sunchokes, roasted pepper and potatoes. Cover and cook for 20-25 minutes until the sunchokes are tender. Remove the soup from the heat and process with an immersion blender to a smooth consistency. Stir in the heavy cream. Taste and adjust seasonings with salt and pepper as needed. Ladle the soup into 4 bowls and top each with ¼ cup of the roasted sweet peppers.

GLUTEN FREE

Serves 4 | PREP TIME: 15 minutes. COOK TIME: 30 minutes.

CREAM OF SPINACH WITH ROASTED GARLIC SOUP

The perfect and impressive beginning to a dinner party, this soup is vibrant green with great flavor. The recipe came about as I was attempting to replicate the creamed spinach side dish at a local steakhouse. It's also the base for my world-renowned spinach and artichoke dip!

Ingredients

1 medium onion, diced

2 tbsp butter

4 cloves roasted garlic, chopped

1 sprig fresh thyme

2 bay leaves

1 tsp parsley

24 oz vegetable stock

2 lbs spinach, chopped

1 cup heavy cream

1/4 tsp nutmeg

Salt and pepper to taste

Note: This recipe calls for roasted garlic which takes about 40 minutes (see Cook's Note).

Cooking Instructions

Sauté the onion in the butter over medium-low heat in a large stockpot until translucent, about 8-10 minutes. Add the garlic and herbs except the nutmeg. Cook for 1 minute, stirring constantly. Add the vegetable stock and bring to a simmer. Cook for 10 minutes to allow the flavors to develop. Add the spinach and cook until wilted, about 10 minutes more. Remove from the heat, take out the bay leaves and process with an immersion blender to a smooth consistency. Add the heavy cream and stir in the nutmeg. Taste and adjust seasonings with salt and pepper as needed.

Cook's Note:

To roast the garlic, preheat the oven to 400 degrees. Peel away the outer layer of the garlic's skin. Cut the top off the whole clove of garlic so each individual clove is cut. Pour a teaspoon of oil over the clove (or cloves if you want to cook more and save some for other uses). Put the clove or cloves on a baking sheet and cover with aluminum foil. Roast for 30 minutes. The cloves should be browned and soft all the way through. When cool, use a small fork to remove the cloves or squeeze each one out. Mmmmm, good in this soup, on toast or both!

Serves 6 | PREP TIME: 15 minutes. COOK TIME: 30 minutes.

CHAPTER FIVE

FANTASTIC FISH, SEAFOOD AND OTHER HEARTY CHOWDERS

I used to hate fish because my exposures to it was muddy, fried catfish from the Illinois River cooked by my relatives. In addition, I went to a daycare that once a week served a tuna noodle casserole. You had to eat or couldn't go outside so I stayed indoors once a week. But now I'm a big fisherman myself. I love the light, friendly flavors of fish in soup. Fish and shellfish soups offer different tastes and textures than the other soups in this book. The sea makes them distinctive, sometimes higher end but always new and different. Fish flavors are relatively mild so we generally don't use aggressive spices in general. We don't want to overwhelm the flavors so we keep these soups nice, light and delicate. (Clam chowder is a bit different since back in the day, cooks were trying to cover the taste of some questionable shellfish.)

It's good to remember for this chapter that fish cooks quickly in soups. Be careful to not overcook it or it will be rubbery. Perfectly cooked fish is flaky and wonderful. And I can't emphasize enough that quality seafood makes a huge difference in the flavor. I'm a naturally frugal person, but I recommend spending your money when buying fish. It will be worth it.

SOUPBOX CIOPPINO

Cioppino is a San Franciscan classic, featuring the bounty of the sea swimming in tasty tomato-based broth. Traditionally the seafood in Cioppino is served in the shell, but for our stores we shell everything for easier eating and use the shells for the stock. I like to serve this in freshly baked sourdough-bread bowls like they do in San Francisco.

Ingredients

1 large red onion, diced

2 carrots, diced

2 stalks celery, diced

2 tbsp olive oil

2 tbsp butter

4 cloves garlic, minced

½ tsp salt

¼ tsp black pepper

¼ tsp paprika

½ tsp thyme

2 bay leaves

3 tbsp tomato paste

1 cup dry white wine

48 oz fish stock (chicken stock can be substituted)

3 tbsp cornstarch mixed with 3 tbsp cold water

1 lb firm white fish such as halibut, cut into 1-inch pieces

1 lb fresh clams, scrubbed and soaked for 20 minutes in fresh cold water to get the grit out

1 lb fresh mussels, scrubbed, debearded and soaked for 20 minutes in fresh cold water to get the grit out

2 lbs jumbo raw shrimp, shelled and cleaned

Salt and pepper to taste

Note: Don't forget to soak the mussels and clams in cold water for 20 minutes to get the grit out.

Cooking Instructions

Melt the butter with the olive oil over medium heat in a large stockpot. Sauté the onions, carrot and celery in the butter and oil until fragrant, about 5 minutes. Add the garlic, salt, pepper, paprika, thyme, bay leaves and tomato paste, and cook for 2 minutes, stirring constantly. Deglaze the pan with the white wine and reduce by half. Then add the stock and bring to a simmer. Cook until the flavors develop, about 15 minutes. Thicken the soup with the cornstarch slurry and cook until the starch taste disappears, about 5 minutes longer. Add the fish filets and cook until just done, about 5 minutes. Add the clams and mussels and cook until they open, about 5-7 minutes longer. Finally add the shrimp and cook until pink and curled, about 5 minutes. Taste the cioppino and adjust seasonings as necessary with salt and pepper.

Cook's Note:

This is an expensive dish but worth it, and entirely easier and lighter than a bouillabaisse. It is hard to imagine that this big-ticket recipe originated from a puréed vegetable soup with the addition of trimmings from a fishmonger.

GLUTEN FREE

Serves 6 | PREP TIME: 15 minutes. COOK TIME: 30 minutes.

NANTUCKET OYSTER STEW

The northeast coast of America has long been home to some of the finest oyster beds in the world, and this simple and tasty stew is an example of the many ways to eat them.

Ingredients

2 shallots, diced

1 carrot, diced

2 stalks celery, diced

2 tbsp canola oil

2 tbsp butter

2 cloves garlic, minced

½ tsp salt

¼ tsp white pepper

¼ tsp paprika

2 tbsp flour

16 oz fish stock

16 oz whole milk

2 medium potatoes, peeled and diced

1 lb freshly shucked oysters, with their liquor (about 35-40 oysters)

¼ cup heavy cream

Salt and pepper to taste

GLUTEN FREE

Cooking Instructions

Sauté the shallots, carrots and the celery in the canola oil and butter in a large stockpot set over medium heat until fragrant, about 5 minutes. Add the garlic, salt, pepper, paprika and flour, and cook for 5 minutes, stirring constantly. Add the stock and milk, and bring to a simmer. Add the potatoes and cook for 15 minutes. The soup will thicken as the potatoes cook. Add the oysters and their liquor, cook until the edges curl and they are just done, about 5 minutes. Remove from the heat and stir in the cream. Adjust seasonings as necessary with salt and pepper.

Cook's Note:

I like to use Wellfleet oysters for this recipe. They tend to have deep cups which allow one to preserve as much of the oyster liquor as possible when shucking. Canned oysters can be substituted, but aren't as flavorful for this stew.

Serves 4 | PREP TIME: 10 minutes. COOK TIME: 35 minutes.

NEW ENGLAND CLAM CHOWDER

This is our take on a regional classic favorite. Clam chowder is just great, so why mess with it, I say. Use high-quality seafood; it makes a big difference.

Ingredients

5 lbs fresh sea clams or 2 lbs clam meat, chopped. Allow the clams to sit in fresh water for 20 minutes to get the sand out

1 medium onion, diced

2 stalks celery, diced

4 oz salt pork, medium diced

1 clove garlic, minced

1 sprig fresh thyme

1 bay leaf

¼ cup white wine

24 oz clam broth (chicken or fish stock can be substituted)

3 medium potatoes, diced

1 tbsp cornstarch mixed with 2 tbsp water

1 cup heavy cream

Salt and pepper to taste

Note: Don't forget to soak the mussels and clams in cold water for 20 minutes to get the grit out.

Cooking Instructions

Steam fresh clams until just opened, about 4 minutes. Shuck the clams and then chop and set aside. Be careful to reserve any liquid from the clams (note: if using precooked or canned clams skip to next step). Sauté the salt pork in a large stockpot over medium heat for 5 minutes. Add the onion, celery and garlic, and cook for another 8 minutes until translucent. Add the fresh thyme and bay leaf, and cook for another 5 minutes. Deglaze the pan with white wine and reduce the liquid for 3 minutes. Add the clam broth and bring the chowder to a simmer. Add the potatoes and cook for another 15 minutes until they are fork tender. Add the cornstarch and allow the chowder to thicken, about 5 minutes. Remove from heat. Remove the thyme and the bay leaf, and add the clams and heavy cream. Taste and adjust seasonings with salt and pepper as needed.

Serves 4 | PREP TIME: 15 minutes. COOK TIME: 30 minutes.

MARYLAND CRAB CHOWDER

This simple East Coast classic comes together quickly and is lighter than most chowders in a nice way. Some crusty sourdough bread and a cold beer make this a perfect dinner.

Ingredients

2 shallots, diced

2 stalks celery, diced

2 tbsp canola oil

2 cloves garlic, minced

½ tsp salt

¼ tsp white pepper

¼ tsp paprika

¼ tsp red chili flakes

16 oz fish stock

16 oz whole milk

2 medium potatoes, peeled and diced

1 lb lump crab meat, picked over to remove shells

1 cup corn kernels, fresh or frozen

½ cup English peas, fresh or frozen

1 tbsp cornstarch mixed with 1 tbsp cold milk

Salt and pepper to taste

GLUTEN FREE

Cooking Instructions

Sauté the shallots and celery in the canola oil in a large stockpot set over medium heat until fragrant, about 5 minutes. Add the garlic, salt, pepper, paprika and chili flakes, and cook for 2 minutes, stirring constantly. Add the stock and milk, and bring to a simmer. Then add the potatoes and cook for 15 minutes until tender. Add the crab meat, corn and peas, and cook until warmed through, about 5 minutes. Thicken the chowder with the cornstarch slurry, being sure to cook the starch taste out, 5 more minutes. Adjust seasonings as necessary with salt and pepper.

Cook's Note:

This is one of the best uses for leftover crab meat ever, besides maybe crab cakes which I love.

Serves 4 | PREP TIME: 10 minutes. COOK TIME: 35 minutes.

ALASKAN KING CRAB & SWEET CORN CHOWDER

The origin of this recipe is simple; I had served king-crab legs the night before and had quite a bit of leftovers. The larger pieces went into a stir-fry, but all the tasty but small pieces from the ends of the legs and joints went into this soup. It turned out so tasty, we added it to the stores' menus. The sweetness of the crab and corn is nicely balanced with potatoes and paprika, then smoothed with a bit of cream, a winning combination.

Ingredients

2 shallots, diced

2 stalks celery, diced

1 carrot, diced

1 tbsp olive oil

2 cloves garlic, minced

½ tsp Old Bay Seasoning

¼ tsp salt

¼ tsp black pepper

¼ tsp paprika

¼ tsp thyme

2 bay leaves

1 cup dry white wine

24 oz fish stock (chicken stock can be substituted)

3 medium Yukon gold potatoes, diced

2 tbsp cornstarch mixed with 2 tbsp cold milk

1 ½ lbs Alaskan king crab meat, shelled and cleaned

1 cup sweet corn kernels, fresh or frozen

8 oz heavy cream

Salt and pepper to taste

Fresh parsley, chopped for garnish

Cooking Instructions

Sauté the shallots, carrot and celery in the oil in a large stockpot set over medium heat until fragrant, about 5 minutes. Add the garlic, Old Bay Seasoning, salt, pepper, paprika, thyme and bay leaves, and cook for 2 minutes, stirring constantly. Deglaze the pan with the white wine and reduce by half. Add the stock and bring to a simmer. Add the potatoes and cook until tender, about 15 minutes. Thicken with the cornstarch slurry and cook until the starch taste disappears, about 5 minutes longer. Add the crab meat and corn. Cook until warmed through, about 5 minutes. Stir in the heavy cream and remove immediately from heat. Taste and adjust seasonings as necessary with salt and pepper. Garnish with fresh parsley.

GLUTEN FREE

Serves 6 | PREP TIME: 15 minutes. COOK TIME: 30 minutes.

HEALTHY HALIBUT CHOWDER

Halibut is one of my favorite fishes and I was looking for a unique and healthy chowder to add to our rotating menu list. This dish has all the flavor of a traditional chowder with much less fat.

Ingredients

2 shallots, diced
2 stalks celery, diced
1 carrot, diced
1 tbsp olive oil
2 cloves garlic, minced
½ tsp salt
¼ tsp black pepper
¼ tsp paprika
¼ tsp thyme
2 bay leaves
1 cup dry white wine
2 cups fish stock (chicken stock can be substituted)
1 cup skim milk
2 potatoes, peeled and diced
2 tbsp cornstarch mixed with 2 tbsp cold milk
2 lbs halibut filet, cut into 1-inch chunks
Salt and pepper to taste
Fresh parsley, chopped for garnish

GLUTEN FREE

Cooking Instructions

Sauté the shallots, carrot and celery in the oil in a large stockpot set over medium heat until fragrant, about 5 minutes. Add the garlic, salt, pepper, paprika, thyme and bay leaves, and cook for 2 minutes, stirring constantly. Deglaze the pan with the white wine and reduce by half. Add the stock and milk, and bring to a simmer. Add the potatoes and cook until tender, about 10 minutes. Thicken with the cornstarch slurry and cook until the starch taste disappears, about 5 minutes. Add the halibut and cook until just done, about 5-7 minutes longer. Taste the chowder and adjust seasonings as necessary with salt and pepper. Garnish with fresh parsley.

Cook's Note:

Thickening with a cornstarch slurry can not only make any soup healthier (as opposed to thickening with a butter-based roux), but it also makes it gluten free!

Serves 6 - 8 | PREP TIME: 15 minutes. COOK TIME: 35 minutes.

CAJUN CRAWFISH CHOWDER

A lively chowder inspired by the time I spent in New Orleans. It features all the bold flavors you'd expect in Cajun cooking along with a bit of cream to add richness and character.

Ingredients

½ lb bacon

1 large red onion, diced

1 green pepper, diced

2 stalks celery, diced

2 tbsp butter

2 cloves garlic, minced

½ tsp salt

¼ tsp cayenne pepper

¼ tsp paprika

¼ tsp oregano

1 cup dry white wine

32 oz fish stock

2 medium red potatoes, peeled and diced

1 lb crawfish tails, cleaned

1 cup corn kernels, fresh or frozen

1 tbsp cornstarch mixed with 1 tbsp cold milk

1 cup heavy cream

Salt and pepper to taste

Cooking Instructions

Cook the bacon in a large stockpot set over medium heat until browned and crispy, about 10 minutes. Remove bacon to drain on paper towels and then crumble. Add the butter to the pan and sauté the onion, green pepper and celery until fragrant, about 5 minutes. Add the garlic, salt, cayenne pepper, paprika and oregano, and cook for 2 minutes, stirring constantly. Deglaze the pan with the white wine and reduce by half. Add the stock and bring to a simmer. Add the potatoes and cook until tender, about 10 minutes. Add the crawfish, corn and crumbled bacon, and cook until the crawfish tails are warmed through, about 10 minutes longer. Thicken with the cornstarch slurry, making sure to cook out the starch taste, about 5 minutes longer. Stir in the heavy cream and immediately remove from heat. Taste and adjust seasonings as necessary with salt and pepper.

GLUTEN
FREE

Serves 4 | PREP TIME: 15 minutes. COOK TIME: 30 minutes.

CREOLE SHRIMP BISQUE

This is one of my favorite soups to serve in a bread bowl for guests because it looks and tastes fantastic. If you love shrimp, that is.

Ingredients

2 shallots, diced

1 green pepper, diced

2 stalks celery, diced

1 tbsp olive

2 cloves garlic, minced

½ tsp salt

¼ tsp cayenne pepper

¼ tsp paprika

¼ tsp thyme

¼ tsp oregano

1 tbsp tomato paste

2 bay leaves

1 cup dry white wine

24 oz fish stock (chicken stock can be substituted)

2 tbsp cornstarch mixed with 2 tbsp cold milk

1 ½ lbs jumbo raw shrimp, shelled and cleaned

8 oz heavy cream

Salt and pepper to taste

Fresh parsley, chopped for garnish

GLUTEN FREE

Cooking Instructions

Sauté the shallots, green pepper and celery in the oil in a large stockpot set over medium heat until fragrant, about 5 minutes. Add the garlic, salt, cayenne pepper, paprika, thyme, oregano, tomato paste and bay leaves, and cook for 2 minutes, stirring constantly. Deglaze the pan with the white wine and reduce by half. Add the stock, bring to a simmer and then cook for 10 minutes to allow the flavors to develop. Thicken with the cornstarch slurry and cook until the starch taste disappears, about 5 minutes longer. I recommend pulsing this with an immersion blender to make the soup smoother. Add the shrimp and cook until they curl, turn pink and are just done, about 5-7 minutes. Stir in the heavy cream and remove immediately from heat. Taste and adjust seasonings as necessary with salt and pepper. Garnish with fresh parsley and serve.

Cook's Note:

I usually blend this entire soup with the immersion blender so it's silky smooth as a bisque should be.

Serves 6 | PREP TIME: 15 minutes. COOK TIME: 35 minutes.

BIG OCCASION BOUILLABAISSE

This recipe takes some time but is well worth it for a special occasion. Break out the nice china and candles, and open a bottle of good wine. Tonight you're getting fancy!

Ingredients

2 shallots, diced

2 leeks, root and top greens removed, sliced

1 head fennel, thinly sliced with fronds reserved for garnish

2 stalks celery, diced

2 tbsp olive oil

2 cloves garlic, minced

½ tsp salt

¼ tsp white pepper

¼ tsp paprika

¼ tsp thyme

2 bay leaves

¼ tsp red chili flakes

2 cups dry white wine

¼ tsp saffron

64 oz fish stock

3 tomatoes, chopped

1 lb firm white fleshed fish such as swordfish, monkfish and/or cod, cut into 1-inch chunks

½ lb clams, scrubbed and soaked for 20 minutes in fresh cold water to get the grit out

½ lb mussels, scrubbed, debearded and soaked for 20 minutes in fresh cold water to get the grit out

½ lb shrimp, shelled and cleaned

Salt and pepper to taste

Fennel fronds to garnish

Note: Don't forget to put the mussels and clams in cold water for 20 minutes to get the grit out.

Cooking Instructions

Sauté the shallots, leeks, fennel and celery in the canola oil in a large stockpot set over medium heat until fragrant, about 5 minutes. Add the garlic, salt, pepper, paprika, thyme, bay leaves and chili flakes to the pot. Cook for 2 minutes, stirring constantly. Deglaze the pan with the white wine and reduce by half. Add the saffron, stock and tomatoes, and bring to a simmer. Add the fish filets and cook until just done, about 5 minutes. Add the clams and mussels, and cook until they open, about 5-7 minutes longer. Finally add the shrimp and cook until pink and curled, about 5 minutes. Taste the bouillabaisse and adjust seasonings as necessary with salt and pepper. Garnish with fennel fronds.

Cook's Note:

For a large party you can remove the seafood to a platter and serve the broth alongside. For individual servings ladle the seafood into equal portions in bowls and then top with broth.

I like to serve this dish with crostini which are traditionally spread with a rouille, a homemade mayonnaise mixed with a bit more saffron and some tomato paste. Here's the recipe:

1 cup mayonnaise
Pinch of saffron threads
1 tbsp tomato paste
1 tsp red chili flakes

GLUTEN FREE

Serves 8 | PREP TIME: 30 minutes. COOK TIME: 45 minutes.

CURRIED SHRIMP SOUP WITH MANGO

In this well-balanced Asian soup, pungent curry powder and sharp lemongrass meet a nice sweet mango. It's a nice and refreshingly different flavor combination and a hearty soup, more like a spicy stew.

Ingredients

1 large red onion, diced

4 stalks celery, sliced

2 tbsp olive oil

2 cloves garlic, minced

1 one inch piece fresh ginger, peeled and sliced

½ tsp salt

1 tbsp mild yellow curry powder (unless you want it really spicy)

¼ tsp ground allspice

½ tsp cumin

1 stalk lemongrass, pounded and cut into 1 inch pieces

¼ tsp pepper

32oz fish stock

1 tbsp brown sugar

1 tbsp Worcestershire sauce

2 fresh ripe mangoes, peeled and diced

2 lbs jumbo raw shrimp, shelled and cleaned

Salt and pepper to taste

Sliced fresh scallions for garnish

Cooking Instructions

Sauté the onion and celery in the olive oil in a large stockpot set over medium heat until fragrant, about 5 minutes. Add the garlic, ginger, salt, curry powder, allspice, cumin, lemongrass and pepper, and cook for 2 minutes, stirring constantly. Add the stock, brown sugar and Worcestershire sauce, and bring to a simmer. Add the diced mango and cook for 15 minutes. Add the shrimp and cook until they curl, turn pink and are just done, about 5-7 minutes. Remove from the heat and adjust seasonings as necessary with salt and pepper.

Serve soup in large deep bowls, measuring 4-5 shrimp per bowl. Garnish with scallions.

Cook's Notes:

Another recipe inspired by a friend. This came to me after eating a Caribbean-meets-Thai type curried shrimp dish he made. He garnished the plates with mango slices. I put them together and added my own touches with a bit of allspice and lemongrass. I like the interplay between the sweet mango and the deeply savory curry powder with the hint of citrus from the lemongrass

Serves 8 | PREP TIME: 15 minutes. COOK TIME: 30 minutes.

INDONESIAN CRAB SOUP WITH LEMONGRASS

Crab is my favorite crustacean. It's the perfect blend of rich flavor and sweetness without the price tag of lobster. This is one of many recipes I spent a year developing to get it just right. It comes together quickly with just a few ingredients, but it's a knockout dish that can be served as a first course or stand-alone entrée.

Ingredients

2 shallots, diced
1 stalk celery, sliced
1 carrot, diced
1 tbsp olive oil
2 cloves garlic, minced
1 1-inch piece fresh ginger, peeled and diced
1 tbsp tomato paste
½ tsp salt
¼ tsp white pepper
32 oz fish stock
1 stalk lemongrass, smashed and cut into 2-inch pieces
1 lb crab meat, (preferably from Dungeness crab), picked over to remove shell pieces
Salt and pepper to taste
Sliced fresh scallions for garnish

GLUTEN FREE

Cooking Instructions

Sauté the shallot, celery and carrot in the olive oil in a large stockpot set over medium heat until fragrant, about 5 minutes. Add the garlic, ginger, tomato paste, salt and pepper, and cook for 2 minutes, stirring constantly. Add the stock and lemongrass, and bring to a simmer. Cook for 15 minutes to allow the flavors to develop. Add the crab meat and warm through, about 5 minutes. Remove from the heat and adjust seasonings as necessary with salt and pepper.

Cook's Note:

Whole crabs can be used in this recipe, and it's even better that way. Increase the fish stock to 48 ounces and add the cleaned crabs directly to the pot. Then increase the simmer time to 25 minutes. Remove the cooked crabs and allow to cool before removing the meat and adding it back into the soup.

Serves 4 | PREP TIME: 15 minutes. COOK TIME: 20 minutes.

CLASSIC SHE-CRAB SOUP

This wonderful recipe comes to us from the southeastern coast of America, but it's famous all over the country. Traditionally it was made from only female crabs. People thought the meat from the smaller females was sweeter. Crab roe used to be included but in an effort to reduce the impact on crab populations, we now omit it. The touch of sherry at the end really sets off the richness.

Ingredients

4 tbsp butter
2 shallots, diced
2 stalks celery, diced
2 cloves garlic, minced
½ tsp salt
¼ tsp mace
¼ tsp paprika
¼ tsp thyme
¼ tsp pepper
3 tbsp flour
16 oz fish stock
16 oz milk
1 tbsp tomato paste
1 lb crab meat, shelled and cleaned
8 oz heavy cream
Salt and pepper to taste
4 tbsp dry sherry

Cooking Instructions

Melt the butter in a large stockpot set over medium heat. Sauté the shallots and celery in the butter until fragrant, about 5 minutes. Add the garlic, salt, mace, paprika, thyme and pepper, and cook for 2 minutes, stirring constantly. Add the flour and cook for another 5 minutes, stirring constantly so the roux doesn't burn. Pour in the stock and milk all at once, and bring to a simmer. Add tomato paste. Cook for 15 minutes to thicken the soup. Add the crab and warm through, about 5 minutes. Remove from the heat and stir in the cream. Adjust seasonings as necessary with salt and pepper.

Ladle into bowls and top each bowl with a spoonful of sherry.

Cook's Note:

I had this while traveling and loved it. I must admit that omitting the roe changes the soup dramatically, but it's what must be done to protect the crab populations.

Serves 4 | PREP TIME: 15 minutes. COOK TIME: 30 minutes.

HOT & SOUR SOUP (TOM YUM)

Tom Yum is a flavorful and warming Thai soup that's become popular all over the world. Though sourcing ingredients can be tricky, the soup is super quick, simple to make and very delicious. Serve this with a salad as a nice balanced lunch.

Ingredients

32 oz chicken stock

1 1-inch piece fresh ginger, peeled and sliced

2 cloves garlic, minced

1 stalk lemongrass, pounded and sliced into 2-inch pieces

3 Thai bird chiles, crushed

4 oz mushrooms, sliced (note: canned straw mushrooms can be used)

2 tbsp fish sauce

1 tbsp chili sauce

½ tsp salt

4 kaffir lime leaves

1 lb jumbo raw shrimp, shelled and cleaned

4 tbsp lime juice

Minced fresh scallions and cilantro leaves for garnish

Cooking Instructions

Heat the chicken broth in a large stockpot set over medium heat for 5 minutes. Add the ginger, garlic, lemongrass and Thai bird chiles, and bring to a simmer. Add the mushrooms, fish sauce, chili sauce, salt and kaffir lime leaves, and cook for 15 minutes. Add the shrimp and cook until they curl, turn pink and are just done, about 5-7 minutes. Remove from the heat, add the lime juice and adjust seasonings as necessary with salt and pepper. Garnish with scallions and cilantro, and serve.

Cook's Note:

This is my wife's recipe really, I like mine with a little more lime juice and less fish sauce. The hard-to-get ingredients can be found at specialty stores online or at your local Asian market. We get our spices for the stores at The Spice House. It's a great store (they have a few in the Midwest) with a strong online presence.

Serves 4 | PREP TIME: 10 minutes. COOK TIME: 25 minutes.

SWEET & SOUR FISH STEW

This stew is loaded with fresh fish and vegetables kicked up with lime juice, ginger, cilantro and pineapple. Serve with a cucumber salad and a sparkling water for a great light lunch.

Ingredients

2 shallots, diced

2 stalks celery, diced

1 tbsp canola oil

1 tbsp butter

2 cloves garlic, minced

1 1-inch piece fresh ginger, peeled and diced

1 stalk lemongrass, pounded and cut into 1-inch pieces

32 oz fish stock

1 tbsp fish sauce

2 tbsp honey

2 cups fresh pineapple, diced

½ tsp salt

¼ tsp white pepper

1 lb firm white fish filets, like catfish, walleye or whitefish, cut into bite-sized pieces

Salt and pepper to taste

Cooking Instructions

Sauté the shallots and celery in the canola oil and butter in a large stockpot set over medium heat until fragrant, about 5 minutes. Add the garlic, ginger and lemongrass, and cook for 2 minutes, stirring constantly. Add the stock, fish sauce, honey, pineapple, salt and pepper, and bring to a simmer. Cook for 10 minutes to allow the flavors to develop. Add the fish and cook until just done, about 5-7 minutes. Remove from the heat and adjust seasonings as necessary with salt and pepper.

Serves 4 | PREP TIME: 10 minutes. COOK TIME: 25 minutes.

SPRING SHRIMP SOBA NOODLE SOUP

Soba noodles are made from buckwheat and served all over Japan from walk-up fast-food stalls in train stations to the finest restaurants. There's a good reason for it, which you will find out soon enough—this is a quick and easy recipe.

Ingredients

1 lb jumbo raw shrimp, shelled and cleaned
1 tsp Chinese five-spice powder
¼ cup mirin
2 tsp honey
¼ cup soy sauce

1 small yellow onion, diced
1 carrot, diced
1 tbsp olive oil
2 cloves garlic, minced
1 one inch piece fresh ginger, peeled and sliced
½ tsp salt
¼ tsp white pepper
32 oz chicken stock
3-4 stalks bok choy, sliced with larger leaves included (about ½ a head)
Salt and pepper to taste
1 lb soba noodles
Sliced fresh scallions for garnish

Cooking Instructions

Heat 2 quarts of salted water in a large pot to boil the soba noodles.

Take the cleaned shrimp and dust them with the five-spice powder. Mix the mirin, honey and soy sauce in a bowl, and add the shrimp to marinate while you make the rest of the soup.

Sauté the onion and carrot in the olive oil in a large stockpot set over medium heat until fragrant, about 5 minutes. Add the garlic, ginger, salt and pepper, and cook for 2 minutes, stirring constantly. Add the stock and bring to a simmer. Add the bok choy and cook for 3 minutes. Add the shrimp including the marinade and cook until they curl, turn pink and are just done, about 5-7 minutes. Remove from the heat and adjust seasonings as necessary with salt and pepper.

Boil the soba noodles according to package directions. When the noodles are finished ladle the noodles into four bowls. Top with the hot soup, measuring 4-5 shrimp per bowl. Garnish with scallions and serve.

Serves 4 | PREP TIME: 15 minutes. COOK TIME: 25 minutes.

ABALONE SOUP WITH STRAW MUSHROOMS, GINGER & RICE NOODLES

I first had abalone in San Francisco while on vacation. I loved the unique texture and light flavor so I set about trying to work it into a soup recipe. Abalone can be difficult to source these days due to overharvesting, but I located one at a farm in California that readily supplies frozen abalone to restaurants all over the country (it's also easy to buy online). The pounding and long cooking time is necessary to tenderize the abalone. Do not try to rush this process or the abalone will end up with the a texture of a bicycle tire! If cooked properly, it's great, tender and delicious. I serve this with ice mint tea or Kirin Ichiban and a simple salad with sesame ginger dressing.

Ingredients

1 lb jumbo raw shrimp, shelled and cleaned

4 oz dried straw mushrooms, reconstituted and chopped

1 carrot, finely diced

1 head bok choy, sliced (leaves included)

1 1-inch piece of ginger, peeled and diced

2 tbsp canola oil

1 clove garlic, minced

1 tsp salt

½ tsp white pepper

32 oz chicken stock

1 lb abalone, thawed, sliced, pounded and cut into 1-inch pencil thin strips (substitute canned abalone if necessary)

8 oz rice noodles

6 scallions, thinly sliced for garnish

Bring 2 quarts of water to a simmer in a large pot for cooking the noodles.

Note: You need to reconstitute the mushrooms which takes about 30 minutes (see Cook's Note).

Cooking Instructions

In a separate stockpot, sauté the reconstituted mushrooms, carrot, bok choy and ginger in the canola oil for 5 minutes over high heat. Add the garlic, salt and white pepper, and cook for one minute. Add the chicken stock and bring to a simmer. Add the abalone and cook, covered, for 1 hour. Check the texture of the abalone. If it is still rubbery, cover and cook for another 30 minutes; otherwise, remove the soup from the heat and cover. Cook the rice noodles according to package directions then divide them evenly among six bowls. Ladle the hot soup over the noodles and top with scallions.

Cook's Note:

To reconstitute dry mushrooms add boiling water to a bowl and soak the mushrooms for 20-30 minutes. The resulting broth is quite flavorful and can be added to the soup if desired.

Serves 6 | PREP TIME: 15 minutes. COOK TIME: 1½ hours.

TUNISIAN FISH CHOWDER

This recipe is a great example of how simple humble ingredients combine to make something wonderful.
It is light and full of clean flavors and will have your family and friends asking for seconds!
Don't tell them how easy it was to make.

Ingredients

1 medium onion, chopped

1 small fennel bulb, sliced

2 stalks celery, sliced (leaves included)

2 tbsp olive oil

2 cloves garlic, minced

1 tsp salt

1 tsp harissa

½ tsp cumin

½ tsp paprika

40 oz fish stock

4 medium red skinned potatoes, washed and cut into ½ inch chunks

1 pinch saffron

3 medium tomatoes, chopped

1 lb firm white fleshed fish fillets such as cod or haddock, cut into 1-inch chunks

1 lb squid, cleaned and cut into ½ inch chunks

Juice from 1 lemon

½ cup fresh parsley, chopped

½ cup fresh cilantro, chopped

Salt and pepper to taste

Cooking Instructions

Sauté the onion, fennel and celery in the olive oil in a large stockpot set over medium heat until the onions are translucent, about 7-10 minutes. Add the garlic, salt, harissa, cumin and paprika. Cook for one minute, stirring constantly. Add the stock and potatoes. Bring to a simmer. Add the saffron and tomatoes. Cover and cook for 10 minutes to allow the flavors to develop and potatoes to soften. Add the fish and squid. Cook, uncovered, until the fish is just done and the potatoes are tender, about 10 minutes. Remove the pot from the heat and stir in the lemon juice and fresh herbs. Taste the chowder and adjust seasonings with salt and pepper as needed.

Serves 6 | PREP TIME: 20 minutes. COOK TIME: 30 minutes.

CHAPTER SIX

HEARTY STEWS AND CHILIS FROM ALL OVER THE MAP

Soup is my passion but chili is a fanatical pursuit. My grandmother Pearl made me beef chili as a kid. She was born in 1902 and traveled all over. One of her husbands was a shipping magnate. He would go out west a lot to make arrangements. Pearl went one time and came back with a five-pound bag of chili powder. I swear she used that bag to make me chili my whole life. And I loved every bowl of it.

Fast forward to my adulthood: I love to get up and make breakfast on Sundays in the winter. At the same time, I like to make something for dinner and have it cooking all day. A good stew sends terrific aromas throughout the house and gives your guests a warm greeting. It's just pure pleasure. And that's what stews are for; slow cooking meals with fantastic flavors melded together. The smells are pure joy.

As I mentioned above, good browning is very important for the end flavor. Don't forget to get the pot hot before adding the oil. Do not crowd the pan. Brown in batches. Your browning shouldn't take more than 2 minutes a side. Then you can simmer away with the confidence you are about to serve a delicious and hearty meal.

HEARTY BEEF STEW

Nothing says comfort food to me more than this stew. Slow-cooked beef and potatoes with carrots, celery, peas and a touch of onion; it's the quintessential classic for a cold winter's night. Served with a nice loaf of crusty bread or fresh buttermilk biscuits...heaven!

Ingredients

2 lbs beef stew meat, trimmed of fat and cut into 1-inch cubes

1 tsp salt

1 tsp freshly ground black pepper

2 tbsp olive oil

1 medium onion, diced

2 stalks celery, diced

2 carrots, sliced

4 cloves garlic, minced

2 tbsp tomato paste

½ tsp granulated sugar

2 bay leaves

1 tsp thyme

1 cup apple juice

24 oz beef stock

1 tbsp Worcestershire sauce

3 potatoes, cut into ½ inch chunks

1 cup peas, fresh or frozen

2 tbsp cornstarch mixed with 2 tbsp cold milk

Salt and pepper to taste

Cooking Instructions

Warm the oil in a large stockpot over medium heat. Toss the beef with the salt and pepper and brown the beef in 1 tablespoon of hot oil in two batches, about 5 minutes a batch. Remove the browned beef to a large bowl and set aside. Sauté the onion, celery and carrot in the same pot with the other tablespoon of oil set over medium heat until fragrant, about 5 minutes. Add the garlic, tomato paste, sugar and dried spices. Cook for two minutes, stirring constantly. Deglaze the pan with the apple juice and reduce by half. Add the beef stew meat, stock and Worcestershire sauce to the pot and bring the stew to a simmer. Cover the pot, turn heat to low and cook until the beef is tender, about 1 hour. Add the potatoes and peas, then cook for another 30 minutes. Thicken the stew using the cornstarch slurry, adding it slowly and cooking for another 5 minutes to make sure the starchy taste is cooked out. Add less of the slurry for a thinner stew. Taste and adjust seasonings as necessary with salt and pepper.

Cook's Note:

While browning meat seems pretty straightforward, people often don't quite get it right, and a good browning makes a big difference in the final taste. Make sure to use a heavy-bottomed pot. Let it heat up to medium high. Wait until the oil is heated, you see ripples in it and is as close to smoking, without smoking, as you can get it. Be careful not to crowd the pan with meat, which will cool the bottom of the pot too much too fast. Also, let the meat sit on one side and get good, deep-brown edges before turning. Those little bits of caramelized meat add a nice savory flavor to the dish.

Serves 8 | PREP TIME: 20 minutes. COOK TIME: about 2 hours.

BRUNSWICK STEW

The origin of this recipe is highly disputed between Virginia and the Carolinas, with each state having a Brunswick County that claims ownership. No matter the true origins, the slow-cooked combination of smoked ham, sausage and chicken with hearty okra, corn and butter beans is perfect when the snow is blowing sideways in Chicago (or anywhere else for that matter). Serve with freshly baked biscuits.

Ingredients

1 large Vidalia onion, chopped
2 stalks celery, diced
1 green pepper, diced
2 tbsp butter
1 tbsp canola oil
8 oz Andouille sausage, cut into thin coins
3 cloves garlic, minced
½ tsp salt
2 bay leaves
1 tsp paprika
1 tsp parsley
1 tsp thyme
1 tsp freshly ground black pepper
1 lb smoked ham steak, cubed
4 chicken legs or thighs
4 large tomatoes, peeled, seeded and chopped
48 oz chicken stock
2 cups shelled butter beans
1 tbsp brown sugar
1 tbsp Worcestershire sauce
1 cup frozen chopped okra, thawed
1 cup corn, fresh or frozen
Salt and pepper to taste

Cooking Instructions

Melt the butter with the oil in a large stockpot set over medium-high heat. Sauté the onion, celery and green pepper until fragrant, about 5 minutes. Add the sausage, garlic, salt, and dried spices. Cook for 2 minutes, stirring constantly. Add the smoked ham steak, chicken legs, tomatoes and stock. Bring to a simmer and add the butter beans. Cover the pot and continue cooking until the chicken is cooked through and beans are tender, about 30-40 minutes. Remove the chicken, let cool, then shred the meat from the legs and return it to the pot. Add the brown sugar and Worcestershire sauce along with the okra and corn. Cook for an additional 8 minutes. Taste the soup and adjust seasonings with salt and pepper as necessary.

Cook's Note:

This stew is great made with any and all manner of meats. I've made it with rabbit to great response. I had it once with squirrel at my extended family's house, and it was great then, too. I've seen recipes from the late 1800's that use gallons as quantities, literally, 1 gallon onions, 1 gallon carrots, 12 chickens, etc. That would sure make a lot of people happy and well fed.

Serves 8 | PREP TIME: 20 minutes. COOK TIME: 1 hour.

CABBAGE & SMOKED SAUSAGE STEW

This recipe is simple, quick and deeply satisfying. The smoky sausage simply paired with cabbage and potatoes is a nice reminder that things don't have to be complicated to be cherished and good.

Ingredients

1 onion, chopped

1 stalk celery, diced

1 carrot, sliced

1 tbsp olive oil

1 lb smoked sausage such as kielbasa, cut into ½ inch chunks

½ tsp salt

2 cloves garlic, minced

1 bay leaf

½ tsp thyme

½ tsp freshly ground black pepper

32 oz chicken stock

2 large potatoes, cut into ½ inch chunks

1 head green cabbage, cubed

1 tbsp red wine vinegar

Salt and pepper to taste

GLUTEN FREE

Cooking Instructions

Sauté the onion, celery and carrot in the olive oil in a large stockpot set over medium heat until fragrant, about 5 minutes. Add the sausage, salt, garlic and dried spices. Cook for two minutes, stirring constantly. Add the stock and bring to a simmer. Add the potatoes and cabbage, and turn the heat to low. Cover and continue cooking until everything is tender, about 20-30 minutes. Stir in the vinegar. Taste the soup and adjust seasonings with salt and pepper as necessary.

Serves 6-8 | PREP TIME: 10 minutes. COOK TIME: 35 minutes.

CHORIZO AND SWEET-POTATO STEW

A few years ago, sweet potatoes hit the mainstream. Suddenly all the papers and magazines were touting the remarkable nutritional benefits of this delectable tuber so we wanted to add some to the menu. Its strong distinctive flavor, which I love, was hard to pair with many of our soups. I found a hearty stew paired with this bold, spicy sausage created a real stick-to-your-ribs dish with rave reviews.

Ingredients

1 lb Spanish chorizo, cut into ¼ inch thick coins

1 medium onion, halved and sliced

2 medium carrots, halved and sliced

3 cloves garlic, minced

½ tsp salt

½ tsp paprika

½ tsp thyme

24 oz chicken stock

2 lbs sweet potatoes, peeled and quartered

Salt and pepper to taste

Yogurt, sour cream or crème fraîche for garnish

Chives, chopped for garnish

GLUTEN FREE

Cooking Instructions

Sauté the chorizo coins over medium-low heat in a large stockpot, about 5-8 minutes so the chorizo has rendered and crisped a bit. Remove it from the stockpot and set aside. Add the onions and carrots to the pot, increase the heat to medium high and sauté until translucent, about 8 minutes longer. Add the garlic, salt, paprika and thyme. Cook for one minute, stirring constantly. Add the chicken broth and sweet potatoes. Bring the stew to a simmer, cover the pot and turn the heat to low. Cook for 30 minutes or until the sweet potatoes are tender. Stir in the chorizo. Cook for another 5 minutes to allow the flavors to marry. Taste stew and adjust seasonings as necessary with salt and pepper. Put in serving bowls and garnish with a dollop of yogurt, sour cream or crème fraîche, and chives.

Serves 6-8 | PREP TIME: 10 minutes. COOK TIME. 45 minutes.

COCK-A-LEEKIE STEW

This is our version of a classic Scottish soup of chicken and leeks. We add pearled barley, celery and carrots to turn this into a hearty stew. Traditionally cock-a-leekie is garnished with prunes, but we never had much success offering them.

Ingredients

5 leeks, root and green tops trimmed and cut into ¼ inch half moons

2 carrots, sliced

2 stalks celery, sliced

½ tsp salt

4 tbsp butter

3 cloves garlic, sliced

½ tsp marjoram

½ tsp thyme

¼ tsp chervil

¼ tsp rosemary

32 oz water

1 roasting chicken cut into 8 pieces (about 4 lbs)

4 oz pearled barley

Salt and black pepper to taste

Cooking Instructions

Sauté the leeks, celery and carrots with the salt in the butter over medium-low heat in a large stockpot until fragrant, about 10 minutes. Add the garlic and dried herbs. Cook for 2 minutes, stirring constantly. Add the water and chicken. Bring to a simmer, cover and cook for 30 minutes. Remove the lid and skim any fat or froth from the top of the stew with a ladle. Add the pearled barley and recover the pot. Cook for another 30 minutes until the barley is tender. Remove the chicken from the stew, let cool and then debone it, leaving the chicken in large 1-inch chunks. Return the chicken to the stew, taste and adjust seasonings with salt and pepper as needed.

Serves 4-6 | PREP TIME: 20 minutes. COOK TIME: 1 hour.

SMOKED SALMON STEW

We do a big eight- or ten-course dinner for New Year's and one year a friend came back from Alaska with a whole Coho salmon. I smoked a chunk and still had half of it left over, it was so big. We froze part of it, and the other big piece became this recipe. I was going for a chunky chowder, but the salmon flaked and ended up thickening things up in a great way. The response at the stores was phenomenal. However, it was so expensive to make that we couldn't afford to serve it unless we bought the salmon at the end or beginning of the season when prices are down. This soup is as popular as clam chowder when we offer it. I bet you'll like it, too.

Ingredients

½ lb bacon
4 tbsp butter
3 tbsp flour
1 large red onion, diced
2 stalks celery, diced
2 cloves garlic, minced
½ tsp salt
¼ tsp cayenne pepper
¼ tsp paprika
¼ tsp thyme
¼ tsp tarragon
1 cup dry white wine
24 oz fish stock
2 medium red potatoes, peeled and diced
1 lb smoked salmon
1 cup English peas, fresh or frozen
1 cup heavy cream
Salt and pepper to taste

Cooking Instructions

Cook the bacon in a large stockpot set over medium heat until browned and crispy, about 10 minutes. Remove bacon to drain on paper towels and then crumble. Add the butter, and sauté the onion and celery until fragrant, about 5 minutes. Add the flour and cook for 3 minutes, stirring constantly. Add the garlic, salt, cayenne pepper, paprika, thyme and tarragon, and cook for 2 minutes, stirring constantly. Add the wine and stock. Bring to a simmer, add the potatoes and cook until tender, about 10 minutes. Add the smoked salmon, peas and crumbled bacon. Cook until warmed through, about 10 minutes longer. Stir in the heavy cream and remove immediately from the heat. Taste and adjust seasonings as necessary with salt and pepper.

Serves 4 | PREP TIME: 15 minutes. COOK TIME: 30 minutes.

UNCLE CAL'S RED BEAN CHICKEN CHILI

Uncle Cal is Jamie's uncle who passed away several years ago. We have been looking at chili recipes, right after I had crowned myself the chili king for the award-winning Roadhouse Beef Chili. It's a red chicken chili. Jamie loved this chili, was close to his uncle, and we named it after him. I might even like the chicken chili more than the beef version believe it or not.

Ingredients

1 large onion, diced

2 stalks celery, diced

6 cups tomatoes, chopped OR 3 (14.5 ounce) cans diced tomatoes

2 cloves garlic, minced

1 tbsp ground cumin

4 tbsp chile powder

2 cups cooked chicken, cubed

1 cup cooked red beans

1 tbsp canola oil

16 oz chicken stock

Salt and pepper to taste

Cooking Instructions

Warm the oil in a stockpot over medium heat. Add the onion and celery and sauté until softened, about 10 minutes. Add the garlic and the spices and cook until fragrant (about one minute) then add the tomatoes and the chicken stock. Bring to a simmer and cook for 15 minutes. Add the beans and the chicken. Return to a simmer and cook another 30 minutes to allow flavors to develop and chili to thicken. Taste and add salt or pepper as needed. Garnish as desired.

Serves 4 | PREP TIME: 15 minutes. COOK TIME: 60 minutes.

THAI COCONUT SHRIMP CURRY

This classic Thai-inspired curry with a coconut-milk base offers lots of fresh bright flavors in an easy-to-make and spicy stew served over rice.

Ingredients

1 small yellow onion, diced

2 cloves garlic, minced

2 tbsp canola oil

1 1-inch piece fresh ginger, peeled and diced

2 tbsp red curry paste

½ tsp salt

¼ tsp white pepper

1 can coconut milk

1 tbsp fish sauce

1 lb jumbo raw shrimp, shelled and cleaned

Salt and pepper to taste

3 scallions, sliced for garnish

Cooking Instructions

Sauté the onion and garlic in the canola oil in a large stockpot set over medium-high heat until lightly golden, about 3 minutes. Add the ginger, curry paste, salt and pepper to the pot and cook for 2 minutes, stirring constantly. Add the coconut milk and whisk to incorporate. Bring to a simmer. Once a simmer is reached add the fish sauce and cook for 5 minutes. The soup will begin to thicken. Add the shrimp and cook until they curl and turn pink and are just done, about 5-7 minutes. Remove from the heat and adjust seasonings as necessary with salt and pepper. Garnish with scallions and serve over rice.

Serves 4 | PREP TIME: 15 minutes. COOK TIME: 25 minutes.

DELICIOUS FARRO & CANNELLINI BEAN STEW

Farro is a wheat grain similar to barley, spelt or wheat berries and super nutritious. It's now getting popular with chefs to give body to soups or salads. This recipe is a hearty and healthy stew that sticks to the ribs. Serve with a big salad dressed with an acidic vinaigrette to set off the earthy flavors of the beans and grains.

Ingredients

2 leeks, root and top greens removed, sliced
1 green pepper, diced
1 carrot, diced
2 stalks celery, diced
1 tbsp olive oil
½ tsp salt
¼ tsp black pepper
2 cloves garlic, minced
2 tbsp tomato paste
1 bay leaf
½ tsp rosemary
¼ tsp oregano
2 medium tomatoes, chopped
48 oz vegetable stock
½ cup farro, rinsed
2 cups dry cannellini beans, soaked overnight in salted water

Note: You'll need to soak the beans overnight.

Cooking Instructions

Sauté the leeks, green pepper, carrots and celery in the olive oil in a large stock-pot set over medium heat until fragrant, about 5 minutes. Add the salt, pepper, garlic, the tomato paste, bay leaf, rosemary and oregano to the pot and cook for two minutes, stirring constantly. Add the tomatoes and the vegetable stock to the pot and bring the soup to a simmer. Once a simmer is reached add the farro and the cannellini beans and cook until both are tender, about 30-40 minutes. Taste the soup and adjust seasonings as necessary with salt and pepper.

Serves 6 | PREP TIME: 10 minutes. COOK TIME: 50 minutes.

CHRIS'S COLORADO GREEN CHILI

This is one of my personal favorite recipes, an adaptation of my wife's favorite chili ever. "Why an adaptation?" you ask. Because her recipe will have your lips feeling like two caterpillars made of fire right around your fourth or fifth bite! She continues to insist hers is the far better option, so feel free to double the jalapeños and serranos, if you like to heat things up. I like to serve this with freshly baked corn bread and honey butter to help fight back the flames.

Ingredients

2 large poblano peppers, roasted

2 jalapeño peppers, roasted

1 serrano pepper, roasted

10 New Mexico hatch green chiles, roasted

2 tbsp butter

2 tbsp canola oil

2 lbs boneless pork roast or butt cut into 1 inch chunks

1 tsp salt

1 tsp cumin

1 large red onion, chopped

2 carrots, chopped

2 stalks celery, chopped

4 cloves garlic, diced

1 bay leaf

½ tsp oregano

½ tsp white pepper

32 oz chicken stock

2 cups cooked pinto beans

Salt and pepper to taste

1 tbsp cornstarch mixed with 1 tbsp cold water

Cooking Instructions

Roast the chiles over a grill or open flame until blackened, 10 to 15 minutes. Remove to a large bowl and cover tightly for 30 minutes. Once cool, peel off the charred skins of the peppers, cut in half and remove all seeds. Chop the chiles and reserve. While the chiles rest and cool down prep the rest of the chili.

Melt the butter with the oil in a large stockpot set over medium-high heat. Sprinkle salt and cumin over pork. Brown the pork in batches, about 5 minutes a batch, and remove to a plate. Sauté the onion, carrots and celery in the stockpot until fragrant, about 5 minutes. Add the garlic and the dried spices and cook for two minutes, stirring constantly. Add the chicken stock, chopped chiles and the pork to the pot and bring to a simmer. Once a simmer is reached cover the pot and turn heat to low. Cook for 45 minutes or until the pork is tender, stirring occasionally. Once the pork is tender add the beans and continue to cook until warmed through. Taste and adjust seasonings as necessary with salt and pepper. Add the cornstarch slurry a little at a time to thicken as desired.

Cook's Note:

I prefer to cook this dish in a slow cooker. Here's what I do:

Rub the butter onto the bottom and sides of the slow cooker. Lay the pork pieces in the bottom, and then sprinkle in the spices. Layer the chopped chiles, carrot, onion, celery and garlic. Top with the stock and cook on low heat for 8 hours. Add the beans, warm through and serve.

Serves 6-8 | PREP TIME: 20 minutes. COOK TIME: 1 hour.

ROADHOUSE BEEF CHILI

Nothing as seemingly simple as a classic bowl of red chili can be so difficult. I worked on this recipe for something like ten years. I'm obsessed with chili, have entered a bunch of regional contests, and am proud to say I won several of them. I was looking for a chili that was universally appealing so I use just a few dark red kidney beans and lots of beef, which makes our version extra meaty and hearty.

Ingredients

2 lbs ground beef, 80% lean

1 large onion, diced

2 stalks celery, diced

1 tbsp canola oil

2 cloves garlic, minced

1 tbsp ground cumin

4 tbsp chili powder

6 cups tomatoes, chopped or 3 (14.5 ounce) cans diced tomatoes

2 tbsp tomato paste

16 ounces beef stock

2 cups cooked dark red kidney beans

Salt and pepper to taste

Cooking Instructions

Brown the ground beef in a heavy skillet for 5-7 minutes, and drain well. Warm the oil in a large stockpot over medium heat, add the onion and celery. Sauté until softened, about 10 minutes. Add the garlic, cumin and 2 tablespoons of the chili powder. Cook until fragrant, about one minute, then add the tomatoes, tomato paste and beef stock. Bring to a simmer and cook for 15 minutes. Add the kidney beans and beef. Return to a simmer and cook another 40-60 minutes to allow flavors to develop and chili to thicken. If you are short on time, I've served this after 30 minutes of cooking, and it still tastes great but has more liquid. Add the remaining 2 tablespoons of chili powder 15 minutes before service to underscore the flavors. Taste and add salt or pepper as needed.

Cook's Note:

The finish, when you add a second round of spice just before serving, is called "the second dump" in competitions. It's a tried-and-true secret for brightening the flavors.

Serves 6 | PREP TIME: 20 minutes. COOK TIME: 90 minutes.

HEART-HEALTHY VEGETARIAN CHILI

This fast and easy recipe proves you don't need meat to enjoy an authentic tasting and satisfying bowl of red. We use crumbled soy protein in our chili (like tofu) and you'd never miss the beef. We like to garnish this with a bit of chopped onion and some shredded sharp cheddar cheese, unless you are going vegan, of course.

Ingredients

1 large red onion, diced
2 medium carrots, diced
2 stalks celery, diced
1 tbsp canola oil
2 cloves garlic, minced
2 tbsp tomato paste
1 chipotle chili, chopped
½ tsp oregano
½ tsp salt
½ tsp cumin
¼ tsp cayenne pepper
1 tsp chili powder
4 tomatoes, peeled and chopped
32 oz vegetable stock
8 oz crumbled soy protein
1 cup dark red kidney beans, cooked
1 zucchini, quartered and sliced
1 ear sweet corn, kernels cut from the cob
Salt and pepper to taste
1 tbsp cornstarch with 1 tbsp cold water

Cooking Instructions

Sauté the onion, carrot and celery in the oil in a large stockpot set over medium heat until fragrant, about 5 minutes. Add the garlic, tomato paste, chipotle, oregano, salt, cumin, cayenne and chili powder. Cook for 2 minutes, stirring constantly. Add the tomatoes and stock, and bring the soup to a simmer. Add the crumbled soy protein, kidney beans, zucchini and corn. Cover and cook for 20 minutes to allow the flavors to develop. Add the cornstarch slurry and cook an additional 5 minutes to allow the chili to thicken and cook out the starchy taste. Remove from the heat and stir in the corn. Taste the soup and adjust seasonings as necessary with salt and pepper.

Cook's Note:

If you cannot find crumbled soy feel free to substitute two diced Boca Burgers to similar soy based protein replacement.

VEGAN FAVORITE

GLUTEN FREE

Serves 4-6 | PREP TIME: 15 minutes. COOK TIME: 30 minutes.

POBLANO CHICKEN PUEBLO

The poblano peppers give this soup a bit of heat balanced by the fresh and cool flavors of tomatillos, avocado and lime. Pinto beans add a bit of creaminess to finish it all off wonderfully for a nice variation on a traditional chili.

Ingredients

1 large red onion, diced

2 stalks of celery, diced

8 medium tomatillos, husked, washed and chopped

1 tbsp olive oil

3 cloves garlic, minced

½ tsp salt

½ tsp cumin

¼ tsp paprika

¼ tsp black pepper

32 oz chicken stock

1 cup pinto beans, soaked in salted water overnight

1 lb roasted chicken, shredded

Salt and pepper to taste

2 avocados, diced

Fresh scallions, chopped and lime wedges for garnish

Note: You need to soak the pinto beans overnight.

Cooking Instructions

Sauté the onion, celery and tomatillos in the olive oil in a large stockpot set over medium heat until the onions are translucent, about 8 minutes. Add the garlic, salt, cumin, paprika and pepper, and cook for two minutes, stirring constantly. Add the stock and beans, and bring to a simmer. Then cover the pot and turn the heat to low. Continue cooking until the beans are tender, about 35-45 minutes. Add the shredded chicken and warm through, about 3 minutes more. Taste and adjust seasonings as necessary with salt and pepper. Ladle the soup into large bowls and divide the diced avocado among them. Garnish with fresh scallions and serve with lime wedges.

Cook's Note:

I spent about a year adding cumin to everything I ate. I was looking for something that tasted similar to a bowl of chili but didn't have the red tomatoes or chili powder, a twist on traditional chili both in flavor and color. My sister Rebecca grows a lot of tomatillos (seriously the woman has a vermillion thumb) and always gives us too many during the late summer. I usually make salsa verde that we eat on tacos and enchiladas, but I was experimenting with soups and added them to this one. From there it was just 'what can we name this that sounds vaguely Mexican but not too much like some variation of chili?' Someone said pueblo, and there you go…

Serves 4-6 | PREP TIME: 20 minutes. COOK TIME: 1 hour.

WHITE BEAN TURKEY CHILI

A nice change of pace versus the very thick tomato-based chilis of the Midwest, this turkey chili is light colored and very low fat. Top with some shreds of sharp cheddar cheese and scallions, and serve with oyster crackers on the side.

Ingredients

1 medium onion, diced

2 stalks celery, diced

1 yellow or orange pepper, diced

1 carrot, diced

1 tbsp canola oil

1 lb ground turkey breast

½ tsp salt

3 cloves garlic, minced

2 tsp chili powder

1 tsp cumin

½ tsp paprika

¼ tsp cayenne pepper

32 oz chicken stock

8 oz Great Northern white beans, cooked

1 tbsp cornstarch mixed with 1 tbsp cold milk

Salt and pepper to taste

Cooking Instructions

Sauté the onion, celery, yellow pepper and carrot in the olive oil in a large stockpot set over medium heat until fragrant, about 5 minutes. Add the ground turkey and cook until done, using a spatula to break the meat up into small chunks, about 10 minutes. Add the salt, garlic and dried spices. Cook for 2 minutes, stirring constantly. Add the stock and bring to a simmer. Cover the pot and continue cooking until the flavors have married, about 20-30 minutes. Remove the lid, add the cornstarch slurry and allow to thicken, about 5 minutes. Taste the soup and adjust seasonings with salt and pepper as necessary.

GLUTEN FREE

Serves 4-6 | PREP TIME: 20 minutes. COOK TIME: 45 minutes.

DEEP SOUTH BURGOO

This rich and savory stew is a tradition unto itself in the South. Typically burgoo is served for large occasions when a lot of big, hungry people need to be well fed. It serves well over rice or with a nice loaf of crusty bread. I don't use my slow cooker that often, but this recipe is perfect for it; put everything together in the morning, and it's ready when you get home!

Ingredients

2 lbs beef stew meat, cut into 1-inch cubes

2 lbs lamb stew meat, cut into 1-inch cubes

1 tsp salt

1 tsp freshly ground black pepper

2 tbsp olive oil

2 medium onions, diced

2 carrots, sliced

2 stalks celery, sliced

4 large tomatoes, peeled, seeded and chopped

2 cloves garlic, minced

32 oz beef stock

1 tbsp Worcestershire sauce

1 tsp hot sauce

1 tsp thyme

½ tsp marjoram

1 tsp brown sugar

½ head green cabbage, grated

2 cups corn kernels, fresh or frozen

1 lb fresh green beans, washed and cut into 1-inch pieces

Salt and pepper to taste

Note: This recipe requires a slow cooker.

Cooking Instructions

Toss the meats with the salt, pepper and olive oil in a large bowl and pour into to the slow cooker. Add the onions, carrots, celery, tomatoes, garlic, beef stock, Worcestershire sauce, hot sauce, dried herbs and brown sugar. Set the slow cooker to low heat and cook undisturbed for 8 hours. Remove the lid and add the cabbage, corn and green beans. Cook an additional 30 minutes until green beans are tender. Taste and adjust seasonings as needed with salt and pepper.

Serves 8 | PREP TIME: 10 minutes. COOK TIME: 8½ hours.

ISRAELI EGGPLANT STEW WITH COUSCOUS

This is a light stew, perfect for a summer evening. Feel free to substitute whatever vegetables you have on hand. In this dish, you cook the couscous right in the pot which saves time and adds body.

Ingredients

1 large onion, diced
1 carrot, diced
1 medium green pepper, diced
2 tbsp olive oil
3 cloves garlic, minced
½ tsp salt
½ tsp thyme
¼ tsp coriander
¼ tsp powdered ginger
Pinch of sugar
40 oz chicken stock
1 lb boneless skinless chicken breast, cubed
3 tomatoes, peeled, seeded and chopped
2 medium eggplants, peeled and cut into 1-inch chunks
1 zucchini, cut into half moons
1 cup couscous
Salt and pepper black pepper to taste
Shredded fresh basil for garnish

Cooking Instructions

Sauté the onion, carrot and green pepper in the olive oil in a large stockpot over medium heat until translucent, about 10 minutes. Add the garlic and dried herbs. Cook for 1 minute while stirring. Add the chicken stock, chicken and tomatoes. Bring to a simmer, cover and cook for 20 minutes until the chicken is done. Add the eggplant and zucchini, and cook until tender, about 15 minutes. Remove from the heat and add the couscous. Stir to combine, cover the pot and do not disturb for 7 minutes. Remove the lid and adjust seasonings with salt and pepper as needed.

Ladle into bowls and top with finely shredded fresh basil and serve.

Serves 6 | PREP TIME: 15 minutes. COOK TIME: 45 minutes.

PERSIAN LAMB & SPINACH STEW

Very simple and easy, this stew is sure to satisfy. It has a little bit of curry powder from the Punjab area which has less cumin and a little more ginger for more subtle flavor.

Ingredients

1 carrot, sliced

2 leeks, root and green tops removed, sliced

3 tbsp butter

1 tbsp olive oil

4 cloves garlic

½ tsp salt

½ tsp red curry powder

½ tsp turmeric

¼ tsp Ceylon cinnamon

¼ tsp cayenne pepper

32 oz chicken stock

2 lbs lamb stew meat, cut into 1 inch pieces

2 bunches fresh spinach, washed and chopped (or 2 boxes frozen chopped spinach)

1 bunch flat-leaf parsley, washed and chopped

1 tbsp brown sugar

Salt and pepper to taste

1 tbsp lime juice

Cooking Instructions

Melt the butter in the oil in a large stockpot over medium-low heat. Add the carrot and leeks, and cook for 5 minutes. Add the garlic, salt, curry powder, turmeric, cinnamon and cayenne pepper. Continue cooking for 2 minutes, stirring constantly. Add the chicken stock and lamb, and bring to a simmer. Cover the stew, reduce the heat to low and cook until the lamb is tender, about 35 to 45 minutes. Add the spinach, parsley and brown sugar. Continue cooking for 10 minutes. Taste the stew and adjust the seasonings as necessary with salt and pepper. Remove from the heat and stir in the lime juice. Serve immediately.

Very tasty + spicy

GLUTEN FREE

Serves 6-8 | PREP TIME: 15 minutes. COOK TIME: 1 hour.

SLOW COOKER JAMBALAYA

Jambalaya has origins in Caribbean and Spanish cuisines, mixed up with some French Creole influence; it comes from all over the darn place. Our version of this hearty classic includes chicken and shrimp, is made in the slow cooker and served over rice (cooked separately).

Ingredients

1 tbsp butter

1 lb Andouille sausage, cut into thin coins

1 lb boneless skinless chicken breast, cut into one inch chunks

1 large onion, diced

1 green pepper, diced

2 stalks celery, diced

2 cloves garlic, minced

½ tsp salt

¼ tsp thyme

¼ tsp cayenne pepper

¼ tsp paprika

¼ tsp oregano

16 oz chicken stock

½ lb jumbo shrimp, shelled and cleaned

Salt and pepper to taste

Fresh parsley for garnish

Note: This recipe requires a slow cooker.

Cooking Instructions

Run 1 tablespoon butter all over the inside of your slow cooker. Layer the Andouille sausage, chicken, onion, green pepper, and celery in the slow cooker. Mix the garlic, salt, thyme, cayenne, paprika and oregano with the chicken stock and add to the slow cooker. Set heat to low and cook for 8 hours. Once that time has passed remove the lid and stir. Add the shrimp and cook until they curl and turn pink and are just done, about 10 minutes longer. Taste and adjust seasonings as necessary with salt and pepper. Ladle the Jambalaya over rice in large bowls and garnish with fresh parsley.

Cook's Note:

Jambalaya is usually a multi-step hassle to prepare, but we were able to simply our version and think the results are as good or better.

GLUTEN FREE

Serves 4 | PREP TIME: 15 minutes. COOK TIME: 8½ hours.

MASSAMAN CHICKEN CURRY STEW

Thai food delivers unique flavors and some of the most delicious in the world.
This hearty stew balances spice from yellow curry paste with the sweetness of coconut milk.
It can be served over rice or with warm flatbread.

Ingredients

1 medium onion, diced

2 carrots, sliced

1 tbsp olive oil

2 cloves garlic, minced

½ tsp salt

2 tbsp Massaman curry paste

1 inch piece of ginger, peeled and sliced into coins

¼ tsp white pepper

1 lb boneless skinless chicken breast, cut into large chunks

2 bay leaves

1 12 oz can of coconut milk

12 oz chicken stock

2 large potatoes, cut into big chunks

1 tsp sugar

½ tsp fish sauce

Salt and pepper to taste

½ cup roasted cashews

1 tbsp lime juice

Salt and pepper to taste

Small bunch of cilantro, chopped for garnish

Cooking Instructions

Sauté the onion and carrots in the olive oil in a large stockpot set over medium heat until fragrant, about 5 minutes. Add the garlic, salt, curry paste, ginger and white pepper. Cook for 2 minutes, stirring constantly. Add the chicken, bay leaves, coconut milk and stock to the pot, bring to a simmer and cook for 10 minutes. Add the potatoes, sugar and fish sauce. Cook until the potatoes are tender, about 15 minutes. Check the chicken to make sure it's cooked through and if not, cook for another 7 to 10 minutes. Taste the soup and adjust seasonings as necessary with salt and pepper. Remove from the heat and stir in the lime juice and cashews. Garnish with fresh cilantro.

Cook's Note:

This stew is jampacked with flavor while being more mild than most other Thai curries.

Serves 4-6 | PREP TIME: 10 minutes. COOK TIME: 30 minutes.

SPICY AFRICAN FISH STEW

This is our take on a traditional African fish stew that's flavorful and simple to prepare. The combination of the spicy harissa and sweet apricot makes this dish unique. Try serving it over couscous with a cold glass of Viognier. Picturesque sunset optional.

Ingredients

1 medium onion, diced

1 large green pepper, diced

2 tbsp olive oil

3 cloves garlic, minced

2 tbsp tomato paste

½ tsp salt

½ tsp cumin

½ tsp turmeric

2 tsp harissa*

3 fresh tomatoes, diced (or one 14.5 ounce canned diced tomatoes)

32 oz fish stock

1 medium potato, peeled and diced

4 oz dried apricots, diced

Pinch of saffron threads

1 lb firm fish filets, such as perch, catfish or walleye, boned and cut into 1 inch pieces

Salt and pepper to taste

Cooking Instructions

Sauté the onion and green pepper in the olive oil in a large stockpot set over medium heat until fragrant, about 5 minutes. Add the garlic, tomato paste, spices (except saffron) and harissa, and cook for 2 minutes, stirring constantly. Add the tomatoes and stock to the pot, and bring to a simmer. Add the potato, apricots and saffron. Cover, turn heat to low and cook until the potatoes are just tender, about 20 minutes. Add the fish and cook uncovered for another 10-12 minutes, just until the fish is cooked through. Taste the soup and adjust seasonings as necessary with salt and pepper.

Serves 4-6 | PREP TIME: 15 minutes. COOK TIME: 45 minutes.

WEST AFRICAN PEANUT STEW

This recipe comes to us from a good friend named Chinua. He's from Ghana and made this at his son's birthday party. Spicy, salty and sweet all at the same time, this unusual and delicious stew is sure to please. And the ingredients are easy to find! Serve this with rice or fresh rolls on the side.

Ingredients

1 medium onion, diced

1 carrot, diced

1 tbsp olive oil

3 cloves garlic, minced

½ tsp salt

1 tbsp tomato paste

1 1-inch piece of ginger, peeled and diced

½ tsp crushed red chili flakes, or less to taste

½ tsp ground coriander

¼ tsp white pepper

1 lb boneless skinless chicken breast, cut into chunks

32 oz chicken stock

2 large sweet potatoes, peeled and cut into chunks

½ cup peanut butter

1 tsp cider vinegar

½ cup roasted peanuts

GLUTEN FREE

Cooking Instructions

Sauté the onion and carrots in the olive oil in a large stockpot set over medium heat until fragrant, about 5 minutes. Add the garlic, salt, tomato paste, ginger, chili flakes, coriander and white pepper. Cook for 2 minutes more, stirring constantly. Add the chicken and stock, bring to a simmer and cook for 10 minutes. Add the sweet potatoes, peanut butter, vinegar and peanuts. Cook until the sweet potatoes are tender, about 15 minutes. Check the chicken and make sure it's cooked through, otherwise cook for another 7 to 10 minutes. Taste the soup and adjust seasonings as necessary with salt and pepper. Garnish with fresh scallions and serve.

Cook's Note:

Chinua, or Nua for short, is a great friend and cook. He served this dish with something called tea bread, which was fantastic, and you should try it if you can find it. Similar to a common French loaf or baguette, it's a bit more dense and slightly sweet.

Serves 4-6 | PREP TIME: 10 minutes. COOK TIME: 35 minutes.

MOLITA'S CHICKEN FAJITA STEW

Molita was a charming girl from Greece who worked for us a long time ago. When she arrived in Chicago she discovered Tex-Mex food for the first time and fell in love with it, fajitas and guacamole specifically. She inspired this recipe because she would make her 'infamous' fajitas for our monthly store meetings. Invariably we'd have lots of leftovers so I began adapting them into soups. After a few batches it was clear I was on to something so I kept at it until we had a suitable recipe for the stores.

Ingredients

1 large red onion, chopped
2 poblano peppers, chopped
2 red peppers, chopped
2 tbsp olive oil
3 cloves garlic, minced
1 tsp salt
1 tsp black pepper
2 tsp cumin
1 tbsp chili powder
1 tsp oregano
32 oz chicken stock
2 medium tomatoes, chopped
1 lb chicken, cubed
1 cup red beans, soaked overnight
1 cup rice
1 tbsp hot sauce
4 tbsp fresh cilantro, chopped
Salt and pepper to taste
1 cup queso fresco, crumbled for garnish

Note: You'll need to soak the beans overnight.

Cooking Instructions

Sauté the onions and peppers in the olive oil in a large stockpot set over medium heat until the onions are translucent, about 7-10 minutes. Add the garlic, salt, pepper, cumin, chili powder and oregano. Cook for one minute, stirring constantly. Add the stock and tomatoes, and bring to a simmer. Add the chicken and beans. Cover and cook for 20 minutes to allow the flavors to develop and beans to soften. Add the rice and cook, uncovered, until the chicken and rice are done, and the beans are tender, about 20 minutes longer. Remove the pot from the heat and stir in the hot sauce and 2 tablespoons of the fresh cilantro. Taste the stew and adjust seasonings with salt and pepper as needed.

Ladle stew into 6 bowls. Garnish with the queso fresco and the remaining cilantro.

GLUTEN FREE

Serves 6 | PREP TIME: 15 minutes. COOK TIME: 50 minutes.

ALAMO RED, PURE TEXAS BEEF CHILI

This recipe is chili in its pure Texas form; no beans, no tomatoes, no filler; just simple beef slow cooked with plenty of seasonings. This chili is perfect in a bowl garnished with a bit of sour cream, lime wedges and a slice of jalapeno, cheddar corn bread. This is also my go-to recipe for topping nachos and chili dogs.

Ingredients

2 lbs boneless beef chuck roast, trimmed and cut into ½ inch cubes

3 tbsp canola oil

4 cloves garlic, minced

1 tsp salt

6 tbsp chili powder

1 tbsp cumin

2 tsp onion powder

2 tsp oregano

1 tsp cayenne pepper

32 oz beef stock

4 tbsp flour

Cooking Instructions

Brown the beef in the canola oil over medium heat in a large stockpot or Dutch oven, about 8 minutes. Add the garlic, salt, 4 tablespoons of the chili powder and the rest of the spices. Cook for 1 minute, stirring constantly. Add half the beef stock and bring to a slow simmer. Cook uncovered for 30 minutes to allow the flavors to develop, stirring often to keep the beef from scorching. Mix the flour with the remaining 2 tablespoons of chili powder and add to the pot. Stir well for 3 minutes. Add the other half of the beef stock. Return to a slow simmer and cook, uncovered, for one more hour (or more until the chili is as thick as you prefer) stirring often to prevent scorching.

Cook's Note:

I prefer to throw the chuck roast in the freezer for 45 minutes or so prior to cooking. This takes it to a firm state that's a lot easier to cut, and small ¼ inch cubes are best for this recipe.

Serves 6 | PREP TIME: 10 minutes. COOK TIME: 90 minutes.

CHAPTER SEVEN

LIGHT, WARM-WEATHER SOUPS

Soup is a year-round meal. When we first started we had a hard time convincing people that it was more than a starter for a steak platter. I'm not sure if attitudes have changed over the past 17 years or if our customer base has become more loyal and interested, but we are selling more soups in the nontraditional soup months than we used to. Part of that is the offerings. We started serving different soups in the summer and have added a nice range of new flavors, and even a few good cold soups to the mix.

Soup in general is very versatile so I'm not surprised that it is becoming more popular as a summer dish. Gazpacho, a cold Spanish soup, sort of led the way when it first became trendy. Now I see soups as desserts in high-end restaurants (and in this book, of course). Soup offers anything and everything. Whether you want something big and hearty, or light and elegant, soup is your friend.

CLASSIC GAZPACHO

Gazpacho is a cold soup originated in Spain that is now popular worldwide. Our gazpacho starts with the traditional tomato base, is thickened with a little bread and comes alive with fresh garlic, red wine vinegar and savory cumin.

Ingredients

2 slices stale bread, crusts removed

1 cup tomato juice

4 large tomatoes, peeled, seeded and chopped*

1 large cucumber, peeled, seeded and chopped

1 medium red onion, chopped

1 red pepper, diced

2 cloves garlic, minced

½ tsp salt

¼ tsp cumin

¼ tsp cayenne

2 tbsp red wine vinegar

2 tsp clover honey

Salt and cayenne pepper to taste

2 tbsp extra-virgin olive oil

1 to 2 cups cold water as needed

Fresh parsley, chopped for garnish

Note: You'll need some dry, stale bread for this recipe to absorb and thicken the soup, while adding a delicious tangy flavor. You can also put some bread in the oven at 350 degrees for 30 minutes so it is dried through.

Cooking Instructions

Soak the bread slices in the tomato juice. Place the tomatoes, cucumber, onion and bread slices with tomato juice in a blender and purée until smooth. Pour out into a large bowl and add the red pepper, garlic, salt, cumin, cayenne, vinegar and honey. Cover the bowl and put it into the refrigerator for at least one hour and up to overnight. Remove from the refrigerator and adjust seasonings as necessary with salt and a little more cayenne, if needed. Drizzle in the extra-virgin olive oil. Add water if the soup is too thick. It should be smooth and thick but level in the bowl and pourable. Ladle the soup into serving bowls and then top with fresh parsley.

* Here's a friendly reminder on how to peel tomatoes in case you missed it before-Cut a cross on the bottom with a sharp knife and dunk them in boiling water for a minute, then dunk them in cold water. The skin should easily peel back.

Cook's Note:

Chicago has a lot of great tapas places, but my favorite is Café Iberico on LaSalle. This recipe is an adaptation of a gazpacho trio they serve in the summer. Before I had gazpacho at Iberico, I thought of it as runny salsa. Their version brought everything into focus for me.

Serves 4-6 | PREP TIME: 25 minutes. COOK TIME: Marinate for an hour and up to overnight in the refrigerator.

COOL CUCUMBER SOUP WITH MINT

Cucumber is one of my favorite ingredients. I was inspired to create this recipe after tasting cucumber soup while on our honeymoon in Mexico. And this is a really fast and easy recipe that's a nice treat on a hot day.

Ingredients

3 large cucumbers, peeled, seeds removed and cut into rough chunks

2 cups plain yogurt

2 tsp lemon juice

½ tsp salt

¼ tsp dried tarragon

¼ tsp granulated garlic

¼ tsp freshly ground black pepper

3 scallions, two chopped, one thinly sliced (the latter is not going into the blender)

Fresh mint leaves, chopped for garnish

Cooking Instructions

Put all the ingredients save the mint leaves and sliced scallion into a blender and purée until smooth. Pour out into a large bowl, add the mint and scallion, and refrigerate for two hours. Remove and adjust seasonings as necessary with salt and pepper. Ladle into bowls and garnish with mint leaves.

Cook's Note:

One of the easiest and quickest soups to make (not counting chill time), this is great to serve as a first course before a larger savory entrée.

Serves 6 | PREP TIME: 25 minutes. COOK TIME: 2 hours in the refrigerator.

CHILLED TOMATO & AVOCADO SOUP

This smooth and flavorful soup is the perfect first-course accompaniment to anything you might be putting on the grill on a beautiful summers night.

Ingredients

4 large tomatoes, peeled, seeded and chopped

1 cucumber, peeled, seeded and chopped

1 ½ cups tomato juice

1 small Vidalia onion, diced

1 clove garlic, minced

½ tsp salt

¼ tsp oregano

¼ tsp freshly ground black pepper

3 avocados, pitted

1 tbsp lime juice

2 scallions, thinly sliced

1 jalapeño, seeded and diced

Pinch of salt

2 tsp extra virgin olive oil for garnish

Cooking Instructions

Place the tomatoes, cucumber and tomato juice in a blender and purée until smooth. Pour out into a large bowl and add the onion, garlic, salt, oregano and black pepper. Mash two of the avocados and stir into the soup. Cover the bowl and put it into the refrigerator for at least one hour and up to four. Dice the third avocado and put it in another bowl, and add the lime juice, scallions, jalapeño and a pinch of salt. Mix well. Ladle the soup into bowls and top with the diced avocados and scallions. Garnish with a drizzle of the extra-virgin olive oil.

Cook's Note:

I love the textures in this soup. It's perfect to serve with some salty ham and several glasses of sangria.

Serves 4 | PREP TIME: 25 minutes. COOK TIME: Refrigerate for a minimum of 1 hour and up to 4 hours.

CHILLED MELON SOUP

This unique and delicious change-of-pace soup that stands equally well as a first or last course. I eat this soup in the heat of summer with open-faced sandwiches and some sweet tea for lunch.

Ingredients

1 medium and ripe cantaloupe, peeled, seeded and cut into chunks

1 medium and ripe honeydew, peeled, seeded and cut into chunks

1 large cucumber, peeled, seeded and cut into chunks

1 cup orange juice

1 tbsp honey

¼ tsp salt

¼ tsp ground ginger

Pinch cayenne pepper (be careful to not rub your eyes)

1 cup plain yogurt

Fresh mint leaves

Cooking Instructions

Put the melon, cucumber and orange juice into a blender, and purée until smooth. Pour out into a large bowl and add the honey, salt, ginger and cayenne. Mix well with a whisk to combine. Put the soup into the refrigerator for one hour. Remove and ladle into bowls. Garnish with a dollop of yogurt and a few mint leaves.

Cook's Note:

I use this exact recipe (minus the yogurt and cayenne) to make popsicles for my daughter. Some people prefer to blend the yogurt into the soup but I prefer the presentation of adding it at the end.

Also, I don't thump or shake melons to see if they are ripe, I let my nose tell me instead. The best melons will be the most fragrant.

Serves 6 | PREP TIME: 20 minutes. COOK TIME: 1 hour in the refrigerator.

SUMMER GARDEN TOMATO VEGETABLE SOUP

I usually make a big batch of this healthy and filling soup when our tomatoes are being harvested and they're coming out of our ears. It's quick and tasty, and can be frozen to save a taste of summer for the colder months.

Ingredients

1 medium onion, diced
2 carrots, sliced
2 stalks celery, diced
1 tbsp butter
1 tbsp olive oil
½ tsp salt
4 cloves garlic, minced
2 tbsp tomato paste
½ tsp thyme
¼ tsp white pepper
2 lbs fresh tomatoes, blanched, peeled and chopped
32 oz vegetable stock
1 cup orzo pasta
1 zucchini, sliced
1 yellow squash, sliced
Salt and pepper to taste

Cooking Instructions

Sauté the onion, carrots and celery in the butter and olive oil in a large stockpot set over medium heat until fragrant, about 5 minutes. Add the salt, garlic, tomato paste, thyme and white pepper, and cook for two minutes, stirring constantly. Add the tomatoes and their juice as well as the vegetable stock, and bring to a simmer. Add the orzo, zucchini and yellow squash. Cook until the orzo is tender, about 10-12 minutes. Taste the soup and adjust seasonings as necessary with salt and pepper.

Cook's Note:

If you don't have orzo pasta, feel free to substitute long grain rice.

Serves 6-8 | PREP TIME: 10 minutes. COOK TIME: 25 minutes.

COLD ENGLISH PEA AND WATERCRESS SOUP WITH MINT

Elegant and nourishing, this easy-to-make chilled soup is a perfect first course for a summer's eve dinner party. Paired with half a roasted turkey club sandwich, it makes a knockout lunch as well.

Ingredients

2 shallots, chopped

2 tbsp butter

1 garlic clove, chopped

1 tsp salt

¼ tsp white pepper

32 oz chicken stock

2 medium Yukon gold potatoes, peeled and quartered

3 cups fresh shelled English peas

1 cup packed fresh watercress, washed and chopped

Salt and pepper to taste

2 tbsp mint leaves

creme fraiche to garnish

Cooking Instructions

Sauté the shallots in the butter in a large stockpot over medium heat until fragrant, about 5 minutes. Add the garlic, salt and pepper. Cook for 1 minute, stirring constantly. Add the stock and bring the soup to a rapid simmer. Add the potatoes and cook for 10 minutes until tender. Add the peas and cook for 3 minutes. Remove from the heat and add the watercress. Taste the soup and adjust seasonings as necessary with salt and pepper. Allow the soup to cool and then add one tbsp of the mint and process to a smooth consistency in a food processor, blender or with an immersion blender. Transfer to another container and chill in the refrigerator at least 4 hours or overnight. Ladle the soup into bowls, top with a dollop of crème fraiche and sprinkle with mint leaves.

Serves 6 | PREP TIME: 10 minutes. COOK TIME: 15 minutes plus at least four hours in the refrigerator to chill.

CHAPTER EIGHT

A WORD ON STOCK

Stock is the base foundation for our soups. Though stock is simple and easy to make, it's important to note that you should take your time and follow each step precisely to achieve the best results. Once you've made a stock or three, you'll be amazed at the quality and taste a homemade broth adds to your recipes. You'll never buy canned or powdered bouillon again!

BASIC VEGETABLE STOCK

It's possible to get a nicely flavored vegetable stock if you give the vegetables some time and attention. This is the stock we use at the stores.

Ingredients

2 medium onions, diced

2 carrots, diced

2 stalks celery, diced

1 large tomato, chopped

1 tbsp canola oil

2 cloves garlic, minced

4 oz button mushrooms, diced

2 tbsp tomato paste

½ tsp salt

½ tsp black pepper

½ tsp thyme

½ tsp parsley

1 bay leaf

1 quart cold water

Cooking Instructions

Add the canola oil to a large stockpot and warm over medium heat. When the oil is hot, add the onions, carrots and celery, and cook for 5 minutes. Add the garlic, mushrooms, tomato paste and seasonings. Cook for one minute, stirring constantly. Add the tomatoes and cold water. Bring the stock to a simmer and cook uncovered for 45 minutes to allow the flavors to develop. The stock is then ready to be put through a cheesecloth-lined strainer and transferred to other containers to be refrigerated or frozen.

Makes about 1 quart stock. PREP TIME: 15 minutes. COOK TIME: 1 hour.

BASIC BEEF STOCK

Ingredients

4 lbs beef bones
2 tbsp canola oil
2 large onions, chopped
2 carrots, chopped
2 stalks celery, chopped
2 cloves garlic, smashed
2 cups red wine
1 tsp salt
1 tsp black pepper
1 tsp dried thyme
1 tsp dried parsley
2 bay leaves
2 quarts cold water

Cooking Instructions

Preheat oven to 400 degrees. Put the bones and vegetables into a large bowl and drizzle with the canola oil. Place the bones and vegetables in a large high sided roasting pan. Roast in the oven for 45 minutes. Remove bones from oven and add the red wine. Let the roasting pan sit for 15 minutes. Remove the bones and vegetables from the roasting pan and add them to a stockpot. Use a spatula to scrape the roasting pan, getting all the browned bits off the bottom and add all that to the stockpot. Add the cold water and spices, and bring the stock to a simmer. Continue cooking until reduced by half, about 2-3 hours, skimming off any foam or scum that rises to the surface. Strain and transfer to other containers and refrigerate or freeze.

Cook's Note:

This stock can be easily defatted; simply skim the stock after it has spent a night in the fridge.

Makes about 1 quart stock. PREP TIME: 15 minutes. COOK TIME: 4 hours.

BASIC CHICKEN STOCK

Ingredients

4 lbs chicken backs, necks and wingtips

2 tbsp canola oil

2 large onions, chopped

2 carrots, chopped

2 stalks celery, chopped

2 cloves garlic, smashed

1 tsp salt

1 tsp black pepper

1 tsp dried thyme

1 tsp dried parsley

2 bay leaves

2 cups white wine

2 quarts cold water

Cooking Instructions

Warm the canola oil in a large stockpot over medium heat. Add the onion, carrot and celery, and cook for 5 minutes. Add the garlic and seasonings. Cook for one minute, stirring constantly. Add the chicken parts and cook for 5 minutes more. Add the wine and scrape the bottom of the pan with a spatula to get all the brown bits. Add the cold water and bring the stock to a simmer. Continue cooking until reduced by half, about 2-3 hours, being sure to skim any foam or scum that rises to the surface. After the stock has been reduced, it is ready to be put through a strainer and transferred to other containers to be refrigerated or frozen.

Cook's Note:

Like the beef stock this stock can be easily defatted by skimming the stock after it has spent a night in the fridge.

Makes about 1 quart stock. PREP TIME: 15 minutes. COOK TIME: 4 hours.

BASIC FISH STOCK

Fish stock is slightly different from beef or chicken stock, namely it takes far less time.

Ingredients

2 lbs fish bones and/or heads (we use both)
1 large onion, chopped
1 carrot, chopped
1 stalk celery, chopped
1 clove garlic, smashed
½ tsp salt
½ tsp black pepper
½ tsp dried thyme
½ tsp dried parsley
1 bay leaf
1 cup white wine
1 quart cold water
1 tbsp canola oil

Cooking Instructions

Add the canola oil to a large stockpot and warm over medium heat. Add the onion, carrot and celery and cook for 5 minutes. Add the garlic and the seasonings and cook for one minute, stirring constantly. Add the fish bones and heads, and cook for 5 minutes more. Add the wine and scrape the bottom of the pan with a spatula to get all the brown bits. Add the cold water and bring the stock to a simmer. Cook uncovered for 30 minutes to allow the flavors to develop, being sure to skim any foam or scum that rises to the surface. Do not overcook or the stock will be bitter. After 30 minutes have passed the stock is ready to be put through a fine strainer and transferred to other containers to be refrigerated or frozen. Be sure to use a very fine mesh strainer or line your strainer with a cheesecloth to keep the broth nice and clear.

Makes about 1 quart stock | PREP TIME. 15 minutes. COOK TIME. 1 hour.

ABOUT THE AUTHORS

Garland Dru Melton has been in the restaurant industry his whole life and started working in the kitchen at a young age with his grandmother and mother, a restaurant industry veteran. He went on to cooking school and then has taken his cooking influence equally from top Chicago chefs as well as his small-town, farm upbringing in Chillicothe, IL that emphasized fresh, wholesome and locally produced ingredients. He has 25 years of restaurant experience and been everything from a busboy to head chef. He is now the general manager of the Soupbox.

Jamie Taerbaum started the Soupbox in 1995 on a shoestring and has grown it into the most popular and best reviewed soup restaurant in the city. It has been featured in practically every major network and newspaper in Chicago, including a recommendation from ABC's "Hungry Hound," and now has a second location in the River North section of Chicago.

ACKNOWLEDGMENTS

Jamie: I'd like to thank my mom for having me and raising five kids on her own. Otherwise there would be no Soupbox. And I would like to extend my appreciation to Dru for his dedication day after day making Soupbox a special place and eliciting thoughts of family, well-being and comfort.

Dru: To Christine, Pearl, Max and the rest of my family. Thank you for all the love and support you provide. To Jamie for keeping a hand on the wheel and letting me run with the ball. To my editor Will, who has made this entire process a joy.

RECIPE INDEX

INDEX

Persian Lamb + Spinach   205

Turkey Wild Mushroom Soup   p 118